# No-one's L
Mothers, Fathers and

# No-one's Listening:
## Mothers, Fathers and Child Sexual Abuse

Joy Trotter

Whiting & Birch
mcmxcviii

© Joy Trotter, 1998
All rights reserved. No part of this publication may be reproduced in any form without permission. Whiting & Birch Ltd are registered with the Publishers Licensing Society, London, England and the Copyright Clearance Centre, Salem Mass. USA.
Published by Whiting & Birch Ltd,
PO Box 872, London SE23 3HL, England.
*USA:* Paul & Co, Publishers' Consortium Inc, PO Box 442, Concord, MA 01742.
*British Library Cataloguing in Publication Data.*
A CIP catalogue record is available from the British Library
ISBN 1 86177 023 5 (cased)
ISBN 1 86177 024 3 (limp)

Printed in England by Watkiss Studios

# Contents

   Acknowledgements ------------------------------------------- viii
1. Introduction ------------------------------------------------------ 1
2. Personal Perspectives ------------------------------------------ 8
3. The Public Context --------------------------------------------- 21
4. Missing Fathers ------------------------------------------------- 30
5. The Reactions of Mothers and Fathers --------------------- 41
6. The Professionals ---------------------------------------------- 62
7. Conflicts and Differences ------------------------------------- 83
8. Implications for Practice -------------------------------------- 104

References ------------------------------------------------------------ 122

Index ------------------------------------------------------------------- 133

*In memory
of my cousin Kathy*
*1953-1993*

*and all our happy childhood memories*

# Acknowledgements

My thanks, in the main, go to the seven mothers and one father who agreed to be interviewed and to share their experiences and feelings with me. I have no doubt that their decisions to participate in this project were not taken lightly, and they may have doubted the wisdom of their judgments as time has passed on, particularly as it has taken so long to get to publication. Their stories were collected in 1993, what has happened to them and their children since then is not known; I hope they have continued to protect and provide the special skill and understanding that they showed me. Many, many thanks.

Although I cannot acknowledge the mothers and father by name, I can specifically mention a number of individuals and organisations who also helped me: Hounslow Survivors of Sexual Abuse, Keith Pringle and Barnardos, Washington Women in Need, Sharon Gray and Child Abuse Listening Line who generously provided contacts and rooms (as well as cups of tea) which were invaluable. Thanks also to Heather Bacon, Brian Williams, Penny Thompson, Jo Campling and Jenny Kitzinger for advice and encouragement in the early stages; and special thanks to Sue Richardson, Jenny Hockey and Alison Leech for taking time to read earlier drafts, and for making constructive suggestions.

My love and thanks also go to friends and family who kept me going and kept me laughing - Mum and Dad, Carole, Janet, Kathleen, Carole, Ali, Maura, Sarah, Trevor, Michele and especially Harry.

# 1
# Introduction

ONE OF my primary motives in writing this book was to recognise and value the experiences of non-abusing mothers and fathers by recording and sharing them with others. It was not my intention to provide a representative sample or any conclusive evidence, rather to explore a range of experiences which might provide a fresh perspective to those interested in child sexual abuse. As a measure of how crucial I felt the contributions of mothers and fathers were to this book, I selected a mother's own words for its title. All the mothers and fathers that I spoke to were glad of my willingness to listen to them as they had all felt ignored or dismissed to some extent or another. Mary expressed these feelings most clearly, and they are her words in the title.

It is only very recently that the views or perspectives of parents have been considered by those working in the field of child sexual abuse, and it is likely that many of these people will *never* have considered the *non-abusing* parents. There are many reasons for this oversight, but even now (late in 1997), government sponsored texts and guidelines fail to differentiate clearly between abusing and non-abusing parents (Cleaver & Freeman, 1995; Department of Health, 1995). Whilst it is acknowledged that, at least at the early stages of child protection interventions, it may not be clear who is and who isn't the perpetrator, this is often protracted by a second oversight - failure to distinguish between mothers and fathers. Once again, despite a number of commentaries and critiques (Hooper, 1992; Milner, 1993; Pringle, 1995, Trotter, 1997) government sponsored texts and guidelines fail to differentiate between the two parents (Ghate & Spencer, 1995; Mostyn, 1996).

The sub-title of this book is therefore intended to focus attention on both parents and shows my intention to present a balance between mothers and fathers, and to offer both perspectives separately as well as together. Most of the material is from a number of in-depth interviews with mothers and one father whose children had been sexually abused, but I have also drawn on formal and informal conversations with other mothers and fathers (whose children have also been sexually abused), and with survivors, female and male; and on my own experiences as a social worker.

The term 'non-abusing' is also problematic. It has been suggested that it has a number of 'negative consequences' (Hooper & Humphreys, 1997, p299). Firstly, they argue that it misdirects scarce resources: oversimplification of issues leads workers to correlate 'non-abusing' with 'non-problematic' and thereby justifying 'non-intervention'. Secondly, according to Hooper and Humphries, the term 'defines mothers and fathers only in relation to their involvement or otherwise in perpetrating the sexual abuse of their children' (p300). They argue that other dimensions of relationships are hidden by this oversimplification; crucial elements in the assessment and treatment planning for recovery. The evidence gathered from the mothers and father in this study does not wholly substantiate these concerns. Firstly it was apparent that the allocation of resources (in terms of treatments, investigations and general professional involvement) was based on more arbitrary factors of availability, prejudice and client persistence, as well as on an optimistic guess. Similarly, the term 'non-abusing' did not seem to result in the professionals involved taking a one-dimensional view. The mothers and father in this study reported very differently about their relationships with professionals, who seemed to understand (and expect) their complex relationships, unsupportive families and different difficulties. Unfortunately, although a range of problems and needs were anticipated by most of the professionals involved, they seemed unable to help in many instances.

It has been argued elsewhere (Sharland et al, 1995) that there are fewer services available for children living with non-abusing parent(s) than for others. It has also been suggested that the 'recovery' of children who remain with their non-abusing parent(s) is less successful than children elsewhere (Farmer & Owen, 1995). The experiences of the mothers and father in this study suggest that this may well be the case, and furthermore, the professional services that were offered were not always helpful.

## Introduction

I had hoped that I would be able to talk to enough mothers and fathers to allow me to broadly represent most of society (taking into consideration social class, race, sexual orientation, disability, religion and age). This was not because it was expected that any significant differences between these groups would be found, rather because I wanted to report on the whole of our society, rather than just a white, heterosexual, able-bodied and able-minded group. However such an unrealistic ambition (given my only resources were myself, with limited time and finances) had to be quickly abandoned.

I continued to hope for an equal number of mothers and fathers however, not only in an attempt to try and provide a balance, but also because issues around gender seem to be so important to studies of child sexual abuse (Kelly, 1987; MacLeod & Saraga, 1988; Campbell, 1988; Pringle, 1995; Kitzinger, 1997). Unlike physical abuse and neglect, which may be regarded as relating to parenting (and therefore located in issues of socialisation, class and the gendered divisions of child care), sexual abuse has been regarded by some as a problem relating to male power and masculine socialisation. (Parton, 1989; Driver & Droisen, 1989; Herman, 1982; Russell, 1986; Dominelli, 1989).

I was not successful in achieving a balance in numbers, and will discuss possible reasons for this later on. Needless to say, I think this 'failure' is important, and corresponds to one of the major difficulties faced by professionals in their work with children and 'families'; an absence of fathers and men. It was also my intention to include mothers and fathers whose children had been sexually abused by strangers and also by people known to them or by other family members, and in this I was successful. I had felt that the experiences might be quite different, in some respects, for those whose abusers were outside the home, as issues of access and divided loyalties might be altered. Similarly I expected professional interests and statutory child protection interventions to be different for those whose children were abused by strangers.

Mothers and fathers were contacted by a uniform letter which was distributed by colleagues who were aware of and supportive of the project, and via a number of survivors groups in the region. The letter and form were designed to maximise confidentiality by ensuring that no-one (other than myself and the parent) need know who was interviewed, and to give the parents as much choice and control (about time, venue etc) as possible. The interviews lasted about an hour or so and were unstructured.

The mothers and father were asked to talk about whatever they felt they wanted readers to know about and understand. I prepared two 'trigger' cards to assist or inspire us if needed and a list of headings to refer to myself if the interviewee found it difficult to take the lead. This list was not used as all the mothers and the father were able to share their experiences with very little input from me. The interviews were recorded on audiotapes and then transferred word-for-word onto disk. Editing of this raw data was minimal; colloquialisms and abbreviations were 'corrected' only when the meaning may have been obscured, and all names have been invented.

The very small sample of parents, and the fact that they were self-selected (in that they were targeted through a small network known to myself, and then volunteered to be interviewed) means that they are not representative of the general population of adults with sexually abused children. It can be safely assumed (given that I was far from overwhelmed with volunteers - particularly by fathers), that most parents do not want to discuss or publicise their experiences relating to their children being sexually abused. It is also likely (from survivors accounts about threats, keeping secrets, victimisation and not being believed) that many parents are not aware that their children have been or are being sexually abused. However these few accounts are of immense value as they offer a beginning point for further inquiry and debate, and on the whole, offer a positive message about care and protection for children.

Not only has this book been influenced by the mothers and fathers who helped me, it has also been affected, in the interpretation and analysis of their experiences, by my own perspectives and prejudices. My bias as a white, heterosexual, able-bodied woman must be significant, and my partiality as an adult in writing (for other adults) on a subject which so centrally concerns children is crucial. I am further influenced by being someone who has no memories of being sexually abused as a child. Whilst I have attempted to provide a generally balanced approach to this project, these factors will have influenced my perspective and affected everything I have written; this needs to be borne in mind by the reader.

I have also had to spend a great deal of time thinking about the influences that years as a social worker have had on this piece of work. I have fluctuated between feeling that this has been intrusive and confusing, to feeling that this particular professional understanding has been helpful. Parton (1989) suggests that although research findings are important 'they cannot substitute for sound professional judgement nor can they solve some of the tensions and ethical dilemmas inherent in this type of work' and proposes that researchers rethink their role. He argues that researchers who work 'with and alongside' practitioners and clients, rather than work as distant experts, will produce results which are much more relevant and much more usable. It is unlikely that my thoughts and observations have not been influenced by my social work background, any less than by all the other essential parts of my 'make-up'. It is also likely that these factors had some influence on those I interviewed (and possibly on those who chose not to volunteer).

One final difficulty in work of this kind, is the reluctance of people to talk about sexual issues, and about child sexual abuse in particular, which is greatly compounded for those involved. Secrecy and silence are two themes which run through most of the writing about child sexual abuse (Herman, 198; Sgroi, 1982; Summit, 1983; Miller, 1985; Russell, 1986; Sanderson, 1990; Bray, 1991; Grant, 1992). Adult survivors and others suggest that many people have no memories of the abuse or do not recognise their experiences as sexual abuse. A lot of them are unable (through fear, shame, disability or previously experienced rebuttal) to speak out, and the vast majority of incidents of child sexual abuse go unreported to agencies of any kind (Hall, 1989; Lew, 1990; Sanderson, 1990; Butler & Williamson, 1994).

Silence and secrecy must also be central to the experiences for those close to the victims, perhaps for similar reasons as for the victims themselves: fear, shame or previously experienced rebuttal. For mothers and fathers very little has been offered to them to encourage them to be anything but silent; the services, like the literature, have focused on the victims and the perpetrators.

Bearing all these factors in mind, I did not anticipate that I would be inundated with mothers and fathers wanting to talk to me (having been ignored for so long), however, the response rate of fathers in particular, was disappointing. There may be a number of reasons why fathers did not come forward. One of them mentioned earlier was gender (and my being female will have compounded these issues) and another reason is probably linked to the broader areas of secrecy and silence already discussed. The traditionally 'accepted' position of fathers as providers and protectors rather than carers, will no doubt also have played a part.

This book is breaking new ground in seeking the experiences of fathers - a group of people rarely consulted on any issue concerning children, and fathers may have been uncomfortable with this new position. Fathers may similarly have felt discomfort at the prospect of discussing such emotive and personal experiences, an activity which, on the whole, men are not supposed to find easy. Another reason may be linked to men's reluctance to speak out about the sexual abuse of boys in any context, '...sexual abuse of males is still a 'secret' for most men (and women) in our country'. (Timms and Connors, 1990, p51). I will discuss these issues in more detail in chapter four.

There may be one final, and most controversial reason why fewer fathers than mothers volunteered to be included. Research has consistently shown that although women do sexually abuse children (Tate, 199; Elliott, 1993; Kelly, 1993; Featherstone & Harlow, 1996; Saradjian, 1997), the perpetrators are overwhelmingly men (Kelly, 1988; Finkelhor et al, 1990; Renvoize, 1993). It is logical to suppose therefore, that a greater proportion of fathers (than of mothers) will have been abusers.

All the interviews were completed within a period of ten months (March to December 1992), which allowed me to remain focused enough to keep in mind common threads, but was not 'overwhelming' in intensity. Those participating found it an emotional experience and at times it was difficult for both of us, but their eagerness to share their experiences was always encouraging.

For the purposes of the rest of this book I will outline some definitions I have worked to, and some of the thinking behind them. 'Child' is defined as: anyone under 18 years (at the time of the abuse). 'Child sexual abuse' is not as easy to define. Parton says 'No definition is inherently and necessarily "correct", it depends on the reasons and purposes for which it is being used.' (Parton, 1989, p 61). For the purposes of this book my definition of child sexual abuse is: any experience which the child's mother or father defines as such. This definition is too broad to be quoted out of context as its purpose here is to accept the experiences of the mothers and fathers participating so that they can be valued in their own right.

If a clear and widely agreed definition of what constitutes child sexual abuse had existed, I would have checked this out with the mothers and fathers I interviewed to test its validity from their perspective. One of the more likely definitions would have been 'A child (anyone under 16 years) is sexually abused

## Introduction

when another person, who is sexually mature, involves the child in any activity which the other person expects to lead to their sexual arousal. This might involve intercourse, touching, exposure of the sexual organs, showing pornographic material or talking about things in an erotic way.' (Baker and Duncan, 1985, p458). Such a definition might well have stimulated an interesting discussion with parents, but on the whole I felt it would be time-wasting and possibly intrusive to the interviews.

'Mother' and 'father' were similarly defined: any relationship which the victim's mother or father defines as mother or father. I was prepared to accept step-relationships, foster-carers and adoptive parents as well as birth parents as falling within the categories of mother and father.

The following chapters outline some of the details of the experiences of seven mothers and one father; examine some of the issues around support or lack of support; attempt to redress the imbalance between mothers and fathers; examine the literature about fathers and attempt to understand why fathers are so often left out of professional practice and research generally, and particularly so in relation to practice and research about child sexual abuse. Further on chapters explore in some detail the reactions of the mothers and father and consider the similarities and differences; reflect on professionals and their practice in relation to mothers and fathers; focus on some of the conflicting agendas between professionals and parents, and within families; and points the way to some implications for future practice.

# 2

# Personal perspectives

THE AFTERMATH of discovery or disclosure of sexual abuse of a daughter or son has wide-ranging effects on the lives of families. The responses of non-abusing mothers and fathers to their children and to each other are varied, but their experiences are similarly extensive and exhausting. It has been suggested (Bennetts et al 1992) that the anguish of the parents may be more immediately acute than that of the children.

The characteristics and details of the parents I talked to, and their experiences are described here. The obvious dilemma for me, both personally and professionally, was and is 'how do I know they are non-abusing?' The only answer, which may well seem inadequate to many people (and I assume that most people share these doubts), is that I don't know. I have proceeded on a basis of trust, but also with a significant amount of experience in this area. I have been hesitant and doubtful in different situations and to differing degrees, but on balance, I believe that the mothers and fathers who helped me with this book, did not sexually abuse their children. As emphasised earlier, the motives for interviewing and the method of contacting these people means that they are not a representative sample, rather a collection of individuals who were willing to share their experiences.

There were eight non-abusing parents included, seven mothers and one father. All of them were white and able-bodied. The transcripts of the interviews contained a wealth of information, emotions and ideas, and all included enough material to provide a crude outline of the circumstances.

The first was Jane's account of events following the sexual abuse of her son by a stranger; (mother – Jane, son – Jason 14 years, siblings – 11, 10 & 3 years, partner – Pete). Jason was eleven years old when he first told his mother, he was about two years old when he was first abused. After years of behaviour problems and emotional difficulties (with professional input), Jane managed to persuade Jason to tell her something. He first told of abuse by a neighbour\friend. Months later he told of abuse by Jane's father (his grandfather).

The second was Alice's account of circumstances following the sexual abuse of her daughter by her partner (the girl's father); (mother – Alice, daughter – Dana 6 years). Dana was three and a half when she first spoke about it; it is not known when she was first abused. Following months of protesting about access visits to her father, Dana spontaneously described (to Alice) what had happened.

The third was Susan's chronicle of events following the sexual abuse of her sons by her partner (the boys' step-father and father); (mother – Susan, eldest son – Matthew 17 years, younger son – Luke 9 years). Matthew told his mother about sexual abuse when he was nine years old, but may have tried to before then too. It is not known when he was first abused. After years of physical and emotional abuse, and frequently suspicious behaviour, Matthew told Susan his step-father was abusing him. Similarly Luke experienced physical and emotional abuse from his father, but as a younger child 'disclosed' his sexual abuse by displaying sexualised behaviour. Luke began talking and behaving sexually when he was three years old. It is likely he was abused from a very early age. Susan's subsequent 'disclosures' to the abuser's family and to the authorities were largely unsuccessful, Luke now lives with his father.

The fourth was Astrid's account of events following the sexual abuse of her daughter by her father (the girl's grandfather); (mother – Astrid, daughter – Ann 20 years). Ann was abused when she was three years old and told her mother about it almost immediately. After possibly only a few visits to her grandparents house, Ann told Astrid her grandfather was abusing her. Astrid reported this to her mother (his wife) who promised to deal with it, but he attempted again. Ann told Astrid again, and they both left the house.

The fifth was Mary's account of events following the sexual abuse of her daughter by her father-in-law (the girl's step-grandfather); (mother – Mary, daughter – Caroline 15 years, step-father – Jim, step-siblings – twins 11 years and sister 3 years). Caroline was fourteen when she told her boyfriend. She was abused for two years before then. Following a long period of difficult relationships and behaviour Caroline, with the support of her boyfriend, told Mary and Jim.

The sixth was Sally's story following the sexual abuse of her son by his brother; (mother – Sally, son – Ben 5 years, brother\abuser – David 10 years). Ben told his mother when he was four years old, he had been abused for two years before then. David was nine years old (he had been abused and abusing for two years before then). Ben had had two years of disruptive and hyperactive behaviour; David, who had shown no signs at all that Sally was aware of, admitted abusing his younger brother (and having been abused himself by a neighbour) when subsequently asked by Sally.

The seventh was Edith's account of events following the sexual abuse of her son by her children's friend; (mother – Edith, son – Darren 14 years, partner – John). Darren was abused when he was nine years old. It is not known how old he was when he told Edith, nor whether he told (or tried to tell) anyone else.

The eighth was Jack's explanation of events following the sexual abuse of his daughter by his brother (the girl's uncle); (father – Jack, daughter – Julie 9 years, partner – Diana, siblings – Peter and Simon). Julie was eleven when she told Diana, she had been abused for about two years before then.

## The families (at the time of the abuse)

Sally and Astrid were lone-carers at the time of the abuse, the rest shared the care of their child(ren) with a partner. Practical and emotional support from extended families varied. Jack immediately sought support and advice from another of his brothers.

> *I contacted my brother who lives just two or three doors along the road. I felt the first and overriding thing I had to speak to somebody else about it, hopefully for help or advice. They were amazed as well, probably 'amazed' is not the right word. Our immediate thoughts were, how was I going to tell me mother? (Jack)*

Only Sally described all her relatives as supportive. Mary, Jane and Jack found their relatives were split, some believing and supporting and others distancing themselves and denying the abuse. Mary described how difficult this 'split' was for Caroline, as well as for her and Jim.

> *I think one of the hardest things for her was losing half of her family*

*at a stroke. And it was hard for me and my partner because neither of us could understand why they didn't at least come and challenge us, or ask us to explain what we thought we were doing. (Mary)*

Jack found that some of his relatives changed their minds.

*By this time there was a great big split in the family. My two sisters, my mother, my oldest brother .... just wouldn't accept it. They just act as if the situation never arose. It's been very bitter, the fact that our daughter's been messed with, she's been shunned by her grandmother, her aunts and three of her uncles have just totally disowned her. My oldest brother's wife came here the second day and she was very, very supportive and cried her eyes out, you know. But she changed her mind. (Jack)*

These divisions in families were described as extremely difficult and distressing, but not always were they unable to be resolved.

*Then we thought how on earth are we going to tell her dad. Up until that time him and my partner had never really got on together, when her dad came to the house to visit it was sort of very cool ... we had many a long conversation ... her dad, my partner and me were very supportive of each other. (Mary)*

Edith, Astrid, Susan and Alice were not supported at all by any of their relatives, at least initially. This position of isolation was extremely hard for the mothers and was seriously compounded in Susan's case by professionals who 'took the side' of the partner\abuser in denying the abuse. Susan, Astrid and Mary could not turn to their own families for help as they had been abusive too. For Susan the feelings of isolation she had experienced in childhood were all repeated.

*All my brothers and sisters have totally disowned us, I've got nobody to talk to. I've just had to handle it all myself, one problem after another. From the age of five I've had nothing but problems. I find it hard to cope with, like I feel my own abuses, and the rape and having nobody to turn to. (Susan)*

Astrid also felt isolated as her own mother dismissed and diminished Ann's abuse, reminding her of their distant relationship in childhood.

*About a week later my daughter said he'd done it again ... I spoke to my mother again and she said it wasn't like that, my daughter had wanted to and she liked it etc. We didn't stay there any more. My mother doesn't feature much in my memories —which is sad (she's dead now). I don't remember her cuddling me or hitting me. I told her once that I thought she'd known all along —she denied it. (Astrid)*

All of the mothers, though not Jack, spoke of immensely supportive friends who would seem able to give any type of practical or emotional assistance at all times of the day and night.

*I phoned his mam up, I was so angry about it. His mam kept insisting he hadn't done it. So a friend of mine's husband blacked his eye. So we let things go by. (Susan)*

*The staff at work have been excellent, all the way through. At least I've been able to go to work and shout me head off, you know. Which has been a bit of a help. (Edith)*

Some of the mothers found these friends and their support through self-help groups and survivors groups.

*I have got support now. Since ... told me about Justice for Abused Children I've been along to a couple of public meetings. Some of the women were talking to us and they were very sympathetic ... they ... decided that I could come to the survivors group. Which was good. (Mary)*

## The families (at the time of the interview)

For some of the families the abuse was still relatively quite recent, for others it was many years ago. For all of them however, the discovery or disclosure of the abuse of their child(ren) was recent—within the last three years. All except Susan are still caring for their children (although one of these 'children' is now at University). Alice and Edith are now lone-carers too, two more than at the times of abuse. Jack, Jane and Mary remain with their partners.

*I didn't want to be turned into, effectively, a single parent who had four children with problems, when I had enough to cope with in a partnership with one child with a problem, and that we all needed to stick together. (Mary)*

*Our emotions were completely shot. I'd lost me mother, I was alienated from a lot of my family, I didn't know where to turn. Diana and I obviously stuck like glue through this... (Jack)*

Alice, who previously had no emotional or practical support at all from her family, now has some support. Astrid found support from her now adult daughter Ann. This was particularly special for Astrid as it was precipitated by her own 'disclosure' to Ann, of abuse many years previously, by the same person (her father and her daughter's grandfather).

*I've since managed to tell her he abused me. I hadn't told her before because I thought she might not like me, and might think she was from 'bad stock' or something. I'm glad I've told her because I don't think she feels bad about me—she can understand better now what happened to her\us when she was little. (Astrid)*

All the others parents report no changes in their families' willingness (or otherwise) to support them, although much may have changed since December 1992 when I completed the interviews.

## About the children

The mothers and father had ten children between them whom they knew to have been sexually abused. Four of them were girls (Dana, Ann, Caroline and Julie) and six were boys (Jason, Matthew, Luke, David, Ben and Darren). Four of them were siblings (Matthew and Luke—step-brothers, and David and Ben—brothers).

## About their Abuse

According to the information available to the children and their parents at the time of the interviews, the children's ages differed considerably. At the time of the abuse, five of them were under five years old (Jason, Dana, Luke, Ann and Ben), four of them were between six and ten years (Matthew, David, Darren and Julie), and one was over ten (Caroline). At the time of disclosure or discovery of the abuse four of them were still under five (Dana, Luke, Ann and Ben), two of them were between six and ten (David and Jason), and four of them were over ten (Matthew, Caroline, Darren and Julie). The children were abused in different ways, all of them more than once, some of them repeatedly over a number of years.

*Type of abuse*

| | |
|---|---|
| vaginal rape | 2 |
| anal rape | 4 |
| oral rape | 1 |
| touching child's genitals | 3 |
| exposure of abuser's genitals to child | 1 |
| masturbation of child by adult | 1 |
| digital penetration of vagina | 1 |
| masturbation in front of child | 1 |
| kissing | 1 |
| showing child pornography | 2 |

All the abusers were male, and all of them were known to the children.

*Relationship to abuser*

| | |
|---|---|
| father | 2 |
| step-father | 1 |
| grandfather | 3 |
| brother | 1 |
| uncle | 1 |
| acquaintance | 3 |

Clearly some of the children were abused by adults who were responsible for their safety. Some of the children were sexually abused in more than one place, and most of them were in what should have been regarded as 'safe' places.

*Circumstances of abuse*

| | |
|---|---|
| child's home | 5 |
| abuser's home | 2 |
| grand-parents' home | 4 |
| other place | 3 |

## Disclosures and discoveries

Five of the children told of their abuse for the first time to their mothers with little or no prior warning or encouragement. Dana (4 years), after months of protesting about access visits to her father, spontaneously disclosed to her mother. Julie and Caroline (11 and 14 years), also spontaneously disclosed to their mothers, although according to Mary, Caroline had displayed difficult and disruptive behaviour for two years.

Ben (4 years), also managed to disclose clearly to his mother, in order that she stop his brother David (9 years) sexually abusing him. Similarly Ann (3 years) told her mother to stop her grandfather 'touching her'.

While I do not suggest that these five children found it easy to disclose, the remaining five had to suffer longer, (the times between the abuse starting and it being discovered was longer in all five cases), and to have many more difficulties. After years of being physically and emotionally abused by his step-father, and frequently displaying suspicious behaviour, Matthew (9 years) told his mother that his step-father was abusing him. Similarly his step-brother Luke (3 years) was physically and emotionally abused by the same man (his father). Luke 'disclosed' his sexual abuse by his inappropriate knowledge of sexual matters and by displaying sexualised behaviour.

*Then when my younger son got older he started saying my dad has me watching dirty videos, and my grandma and grandad having no clothes on. At the age of three my son knew exactly where a penis went, he knew where babies come from, he knew everything about sex. (Susan)*

Susan's subsequent 'disclosures' to the abuser's family and to the authorities were largely unsuccessful, Luke now lives with his father.

Jason (8 years), after years of behaviour problems and

emotional difficulties (despite professional input), was persuaded by his mother to tell her. Her skills in helping him to disclose were considerable.

*I kept on asking what's the matter, what's happened, I just began to feel that someone had done something to him at that moment, and I thought oh no, no, NO. I told him he had to talk to mummy because mummy could help him. He said 'you can't, you can't.' I said 'is it so terrible you can't talk?' He said 'yes'. At that point I picked him up and sat him on my knee. I said 'listen sweetheart, has anybody ever touched you that shouldn't have touched you—a man or a lady —in a way you know is wrong?' He just really, really sobbed. It was very, very painful and I thought please, please let him say no. He begged me not to ask him for an answer because he couldn't tell. I knew then that this is what had happened. (Jane)*

Jason first told of abuse by a neighbour\friend, but months later he told her of abuse by his grandfather as well (mother's father).

Mary felt that it was less difficult to listen to her daughter Caroline's disclosure because she had said something the day before which had alerted and warned her.

*The very next night her boyfriend brought her down and said they had something they wanted to tell us. He said 'now don't get the wrong idea, she's not pregnant or anything like that'. They sat and told me what had happened, which was dreadfully traumatic for her, but I think because I'd had a hint the night before, it wasn't totally unexpected; but I still couldn't believe it. (Mary)*

Not all the children displayed obvious signs or symptoms of abuse. David (9 years), who had shown no signs at all, admitted abusing his younger brother (and having been abused himself by a neighbour) when asked by his mother.

The mothers and fathers also had difficulties telling relatives and friends about what had happened to their children. Jack told his parents separately and found it very difficult.

*I took me dad into the kitchen and said ... told me dad, who I'm very, very close to, what had happened. He couldn't say anything either. So we were just flustered by this time.... but I just .. I didn't know what to say to my mother. Really I hadn't been very ..., I was only just on the very border of speaking to my mother due to problems all over. I'm one of six brothers and two sisters, it's like a train station, there's always people in, so I had to try and wait for a ... There wasn't any other way to say it, so I said 'look, something happened last night'. (Jack)*

## Misunderstandings

All the mothers and the father experienced delays and difficulties caused by misunderstandings. Jane described how she and her partner had misinterpreted her son Jason's behaviour as a reaction to his adjusting to a new step-father.

*At the same time I got together with Pete to buy our own house—yet another dad for Jason. We kept putting all his emotional problems down to this. (Jane)*

Her son was also distressed by a misunderstanding of his own.

*He said that I couldn't take it away, and that he was dirty and gay, and 'I'm going to get AIDS and die'. I said 'no, you're not dirty and you're not going to get AIDS and you're not going to die. (Jane).*

Edith refused counselling help because her son showed no signs of disturbance or symptoms of distress. She believed that he did not need it and misunderstood the professionals explanations and advice.

*At the time of the sexual abuse it was the normal thing because the police involved them, because they did go to court. I actually got a letter saying they could offer counselling for Darren, but at that time we didn't think it was necessary, because I've got a big family myself, I've got an older lot of brothers, and then I've got a younger family. (Why did you not think it was relevant?) Because he was not behaving badly, and we'd talked about it and we didn't sort of try to hide it or anything. So to me it wasn't a problem. (Edith)*

## Investigations and legal action

All except Astrid and Ann were involved in investigations by the police and social services. Jane, Alice, Susan, Mary and Jack reported that there were case conferences held, and Mary, Jane and Jack said they attended.

A broad range of services were offered and taken up by the families. child psychiatrists, social workers and general practitioners offered services which were used the most. There were four police investigations and four of the children were medically examined. Child therapists were also taken up on behalf of four of the children.

Much of the work done by the professionals was highly regarded by the parents.

*... we got a new education welfare officer who I spoke to and she was very sympathetic and she's been very good. She's there in the school if she needs to talk to her. (Mary)*

Advice of various kinds, and professional support were not always felt to be available or appropriate.

*We were never offered a child psychiatrist. My solicitor told us about a child psychologist and compensation (to pay for her sessions). (Alice)*

*The support Social Services offered me all the way through was to put him into care, you see, and I won't have that ... They said that we were not accepting their help, but they have never offered any ... the solicitor said if we started turning down any offers of help, even if I didn't want it (and it nearly killed me to put him back in there), they would go back to court and say that this family is not co-operating. Which they can't say at the moment. (Edith)*

Jane felt that the social worker and police officer, who had undertaken an initial investigative interview with Jason, created additional emotional and behavioural repercussions that they left her to deal with.

*It was too controlled because there was so much emotion in that room—they just left. As they got to the door they just turned round and said 'oh by the way you've got an appointment at the hospital tomorrow for the doctor to examine you and check you're ok'. Well that was a catalyst ....WHOOSH......, but they were gone then. The aftermath of what he had told —I hadn't got it all out before—all this detail to two strangers, I just didn't know what to do. (Jane)*

Susan felt that the professionals could not support her or her children at all, and she continues to press for their protection.

*I know something's happened to the both of them [her sons]. I mean my little one is too highly sexed, he knows too much about sex. A child at his age of three didn't need to know where a penis went, and he knew exactly what it was for, how babies were made and everything, at three years old. I mean I haven't let it lie. Every so often I tell someone. (Susan)*

The timings of the services offered did not always seem appropriate. Jane, Alice, Mary and Susan expressed a need for specific advice following medical examinations and investigative interviews. Jane, Alice, Mary, Sally and Edith would have appreciated longer-term support from professionals.

*... regular phone calls would have been better than nothing. (Alice)*

Legal advice was also not available to Susan and Jane, and was only offered to Alice and Edith. Although the police were involved in six of the eight families, and sexual abuse was confirmed in eight of the ten children, only one abuser (not a relative) was prosecuted and convicted.

*Legal action taken*

| | |
|---|---|
| prosecuted and conviction | 1 |
| police involved; no prosecution | 5 |
| no police involvement | 2 |

The legal system was unable to help Edith, despite complex involvement.

*It ended up, after having an assessment down at ..... (adolescent psychiatric unit), they couldn't take him because of the drug problem. Dr .... found somewhere for him in Manchester which is a secure unit. So when we went to court to get the order for the secure unit all hell broke loose. He was given a Guardian and a solicitor who said he was not going to be locked up. We've had constant court battles since then. We've been in court about ten times this year because the Social Services went for care proceedings. They got him into such a state, he was violent and he absconded three times from court. He was punching the walls. (Edith)*

Despite the efforts and resources provided by the professionals and statutory agencies, a number of the parents felt they needed more support and help.

*I could write a book about there being no help, I think I phoned everybody. I've been right through the phone book, my phone bill's £166 . I phoned the Salvation Army, the only one who did actually try to help me was Barnardos ... all during this time I had no support whatsoever, none at all, I've never had it. Never had any support.* (what would you want to say to professionals?) *Help parents. Much more help and support. (Edith)*

Overall, these stories and accounts provide a vivid and varied picture for the mothers and fathers, as well as for the children and other family members. The families were all very different, with different support networks and different coping styles. Despite all the differences however, there were many similarities - relationship to and gender of abuser, place of abuse, frequency of abuse, and delays and difficulties caused by misunderstandings. These factors suggest that despite the complexity of individual differences and family circumstances, there may be some fundamental commonalities which could be used to inform and improve initial responses and services offered to non-abusing mothers and fathers. In order to consider this possibility an examination of the public context of child sexual abuse is necessary.

# 3
# The public context

THIS BOOK is concerned with child sexual abuse, but unlike many others, it focuses on *non-abusing* mothers and fathers of children who have been sexually abused. As I stated earlier, I believe that the mothers and fathers who helped me with this book, did not sexually abuse their children, but whether or not these mothers and fathers were regarded as non-abusing parents by others, is another matter. On the whole, family identities are structured through social rather than interpersonal processes. The *private* experience of parenting cannot be understood independently of the *public* context in which parenting takes place. A major aim of this chapter is to provide a comprehension of the *public, professional* and *academic* context against which the individual and personal experiences of mothers and fathers can be explored.

Much of the public's understanding about child sexual abuse is based on information received from a variety of sources. Although academic research and literature may seem far removed from many people's usual reading, it informs much of the popular media and many professionals rely upon it in shaping their responses and interventions. I feel that it is essential to examine the literature carefully.

Literature about child sexual abuse is abundant, but material that focuses on mothers and fathers is rare and particularly so regarding non-abusing parents. If mothers or fathers are considered, their complicity in the abuse or failure to protect is usually emphasised. In a recently published textbook on child sexual abuse (Grant, 1992), 'parents' are only considered in the chapter which examines why sexual abuse occurs. Their relevance to the chapter on consequences of abuse, or the chapter on identification of abuse is not perceived.

There may be a number of reasons why so little material is available about non-abusing parents. Some of these are linked to the theoretical principles which many academics hold as a basis to their approach, and will be discussed below. Other reasons may be linked with more personal agendas such as distancing their own involvement or responsibilities by too readily blaming others. It may also be of some significance that much of the research undertaken in this area has been traditional non-collaborative, non-participatory inquiry, which may have minimised the perspectives of the people being researched (Reason, 1988).

Even recent research often portrays a very negative picture of parents of sexually abused children. Grant observes that mothers and fathers of children who have been sexually abused are more likely to have been sexually or emotionally abused themselves as children; are less likely to understand what a 'normal' healthy childhood means; and are less likely to be able to form 'appropriate' adult\child relationships. In addition mothers are more likely to have become pregnant and\or married young; to have chosen dominant male partners; and less likely to have 'satisfactory' sexual relationships. (Grant, 1992).

Not all the literature disregards so completely any references to constructive or valuable contributions made by mothers and fathers, although many writers fail to do little more than acknowledge that some parents do not abuse their children.

The literature seems to have three main approaches to dealing with parents of children who have been sexually abused. Firstly it blames them (either for the abuse, or for some complicity or failure to protect); mothers seem to be especially blameworthy for the latter. Secondly it frequently ignores or overlooks fathers, concentrating in the main on mothers. Thirdly it regards and refers to mothers and fathers as one entity, uniting them under the sometimes unhelpful term 'parents'.

In an attempt to check out a tendency in the literature to a) unite mothers and fathers as parents, and b) disregard or overlook non-abusing and\or protecting fathers, I considered the index listings in some of the literature. Listed in the Index of the NSPCC publication 'Child Sexual Abuse (1989), there are 21 references to parents, 8 references to mothers and 1 reference to fathers. Many authors have listed similar numbers which 'may be indicative of the dominant theoretical (and ideological?) perspectives in this field' (Trotter, 1997, p65). Some more recent texts appear to be addressing these imbalances (Parton et al, 1997), although others are not (Cloke & Davies, 1995; Hunter, 1995) On the whole, the literature appears to regard parents as one unit when discussing sexual abuse of children, and their connection with the abuse, their responses to it and their views about it are considered to be uniform. Furthermore, when it is necessary to distinguish between the two parents, the mother seems to be nearly four times as relevant as the father.

## Child sexual abuse research relating to parents

Waldby et al (1989) point to the reasoning behind the different emphases in the literature relating to child sexual abuse. Psychological literature, they suggest, takes the father, rather than the mother or child, as its object of study because psychologists are more likely to encounter convicted offenders in their work. Their focus has consistently overlooked the non-abusing fathers.

Psychiatrists and family disfunctionalists on the other hand are more likely to encounter women (as mothers, wives\partners and\or survivors), and families of convicted or accused offenders. Waldby et al go on to point out that the feminist literature attempts to redress some of the inaccuracies and imbalances portrayed.

> The feminist objection ... relates to the systematic misrecognition and displacement of the power relationships involved in incestuous abuse; as evidenced by the psychiatric and family disfunction literature in apportioning responsibility and agency to mother and daughter, and by the psychological literature in divorcing the father's actions from any social context....All three perspectives maintain the status quo of patriarchy. (Waldby et al, 1989, p97).

One of the limitations of the feminist perspective however, has been the tendency to 'reduce issues about gender to work with women'. (Hudson, 1989, p70). Not only are women in danger of being over scrutinised and subsequently 'over blamed', men are in danger of being judged irrelevant or, worse still, totally disregarded. '..to ignore men is to ignore the heart of the problem.' (Hudson, 1989, p70).

The feminist analysis of incest as a sexual power relationship has provided a much more realistic analysis of the position of mothers (and children), it has also provided an opportunity to begin to extend an understanding of non-abusing fathers. Their analysis presents two theories; that those of us in society with personal and structural power have an option to misuse it, and those who in addition operate from a personal power base which is rooted in fear and anger, are at greatest risk of becoming persecutors and child abusers.

It is possible to see that although most fathers possess personal and structural power, many of them do not operate from a base which is rooted in fear and anger, and therefore do not misuse their power by sexually abusing their children.

## Research which includes parents' views

Two small-scale studies in the late 1980s included the perceptions and experiences of parents in relation to general child protection interventions (Brown, 1986; Corby, 1987), and other writers have acknowledged parental views with regard to their participation in conferences (McGloin and Turnbull, 1987a and 1987b), their perceptions of casework (Westcott, 1995), their involvement in a special resource centre (Richardson and Bacon, 1991), their association with a community awareness initiative (Cashman and Lamballe-Armstrong, 1991), their involvement in multi-disciplinary assessment (Wyatt and Higgs, 1991), their views about partnership (Katz, 1995; Thoburn et al, 1995) and their part in decision making (Fisher et al, 1986; Packman et al, 1986 and 1989). The study undertaken by Cleaver and Freeman (1995) sought the perceptions of parents involved with child protection procedures and a number of their findings are substantiated here.

The issues identified in many of these studies have similarities: the differing perspectives of parents and social workers go unrecognised; parents may feel pushed aside and disillusioned; when parents felt that their problems and wishes were understood they valued this highly; mothers may be particularly responsive to working with professionals.

## Research about mothers and fathers (rather than 'parents')

Most of the more recent studies look at mothers (Craig et al, 1989), sometimes without even mentioning fathers (although frequently the studies are of father\father-figure perpetrators situations and 'therefore' exclude thinking about father in any other way). Intervention quite significantly focuses on mothers, and fathers continue to be 'let off the hook'. (see Porter, 1984)

This bias has not confined itself to child sexual abuse. Martin (1983) reported that studies of abusive parents since 1976 focussed on mothers in the main and 'a number of the reports systematically exclude fathers and fail to explain why'. In an attempt to develop reliable diagnostic categories or evidence of treatment effectiveness for 'child abusers' these authors simply assume that mothers alone needed to be studied.' (Martin, 1983, p295)

Martin goes on to point out that where some authors do show consideration of male and female abusers (other than sexual), they do not always evaluate the differences between them. Other authors reflect on some of the differences between mothers and fathers, but 'the role of the female parent is still considered primary'. Stark & Flitcraft (1988) have pointed out that in many studies women are often the only source of direct information and 'abusing parent' is often a euphemism for mother.

Until recently the literature surrounding child sexual abuse failed to consider fathers at all (except as perpetrators\guilty partners). Even wider areas of study, for example of child development or parenting trends, have only recently begun to feature fathers (Lamb, 1981; Grief, 1985; Wetherell, 1993; Hawkins & Dollahite, 1997).

Finkelhor (1984) considered that mothers and fathers had a vital role in prevention of child sexual abuse; the differences between them were considered in this context, not surprisingly '...mothers did a much better job of talking with their children about sexual abuse than did fathers.' (p137)

Despite this emerging interest in the separate qualities and needs of mothers and fathers, official policies and procedures have paid little regard to the trend. A report of an Independent Working Party established by the Department of Health published in 1991, admits that there are enormous difficulties in assessments as '....it should not be assumed that there are common interests within families' (Parker et al, 1991, p22). However it goes on to discuss 'families' and 'parents' without mentioning mothers or fathers, and in the recommended Assessment Forms only 1 out of 58 detailed questions refers to mothers and fathers rather than 'parents'.

The Children Act (Department of Health, 1989b) occasionally distinguishes between mothers and fathers. It advocates that family links should be actively maintained when children are cared for 'out-of-home', and that '...fathers should not be overlooked or marginalised' (p9). It does not appear to extend this plea to other situations and, for example, does not alert the reader to the likelihood of fathers being overlooked (and mothers over-scrutinised) when discussing parenting skills. Milner (1992) confirms that the child protection procedures are continuing to act as 'powerful constrainers on social workers to pull mothers into the system and push fathers into the background' (p13). In a later document (Department of Health, 1995), terms used are even more ambiguous, referring most commonly to work with 'families', only once alluding to potential differences between 'adults who are important in a child's life' (p11) and never mentioning 'mothers' or 'fathers' specifically.

The Children Act, which was implemented in October 1991, takes some care over terminology and defines the word 'parent' (and 'relatives') to include the parents (and relatives) of any child, whether or not his parents are or have been married to each other. The Act attempts to clarify and strengthen parental 'responsibilities', which it defines as a collection of rights, powers, duties and responsibilities which 'follow from being a parent and bringing up a child' (Department of Health, 1989b, p9). Other than establishing that mothers have this responsibility when a child is conceived out of wedlock, the Act does not distinguish between parents (although it usually uses the pronoun 'he' when referring to one).

There is some inconsistency in this attempt at 'equality' for fathers and mothers. Although responsibilities are aligned to rearing children as well as conceiving them, the Act acknowledges that the carer 'will usually be the child's mother' (Department of Health, 1989b, p13). It goes on to suggest that the encumbrance of applying to court (for example for an order which would require another person to inform 'him' before a particular step is taken or not taken), 'should not generally fall' on her. Its reason for advocating that such a burden be lifted from mothers is that they need to be able 'to respond to circumstances as they arise', whatever that means.

Others are similarly clumsy in their references to mothers and fathers. Levitt et al (1991) studied the families of 285 children (230 families) where sexual abuse had been confirmed and completed interviews with 104 mothers, 9 fathers and 6 other relatives. The authors acknowledge the limitations of their study in relying on one person's perspective alone—'the child's primary caretaker', and realise that they have not helped us understand cases in which both parents were involved in the abuse. However they fail to distinguish between the responses of the mothers and the very few fathers, they do not comment at all on how the 'primary caretaker' was defined, and appear not to acknowledge that some children may have two primary caretakers—neither of whom has abused them.

## Mothers

A number of researchers and writers have explored the issues about mothers separately from fathers (Byerly, 1985; Richardson and Bacon, 1991; Hooper, 1992; Johnson, 1992; Deblinger et al, 1993) and Hooper's book provides a useful and refreshingly clear picture of mothers as the 'primary adult actors in child protection'. (Hooper, 1992, p4).

Given that a number of recent studies (Adams-Tucker, 1982; Tufts, 1984; Everson et al, 1989) have suggested that a child's subsequent mental health may have a greater correlation to the level of support given by its mother than by the nature or duration of abuse, the role of mothers is clearly crucial and provides a highly charged motivation for analysis. Everson et al and Tufts argue that the correlation between a child's mental ill-health and poor maternal support might be linked to subsequent events. Children with blaming or rejecting mothers are more likely to be removed from their homes, schools, churches and friends, and more likely to experience disrupted routines, court appearances, and other difficulties.

> ...mothers are often the forgotten parties once incest is disclosed. At that point attention usually focuses on victims and offenders. Mothers are too often left to cope alone or to carry the extra burdens of solacing and caring for other family members at a stressful time. The most unfortunate situations find mothers not only left with this usual role of caretaking, but held responsible that the incest occurred. (Byerly, 1985, p7)

They may also have additional burdens of being thrust into new roles and responsibilities (if the abuser was mother's partner) for which they may or may not be capable—breadwinner, decision-maker, witness, or lone-carer. It is likely that they may also be able to reflect and consider many incidents and feelings from the past which now hold significance in relation to the sexual abuse, but previously did not. The resulting feelings may reach overwhelming proportions.

> The term mother survivor is an appropriate term for every woman who struggles, manages, and finally comes through her child's incest with herself intact. (Byerly, 1985, p8)

Deblinger's study (Deblinger et al, 1993) provides a less negative view than many of non-abusing mothers, particularly of 'incest mothers' who were as likely to believe and protect their children as other non-abusing mothers.

## Fathers

One study of fathers as sole carers of their 'maltreated' (defined as physically abused and neglected by mother) children does explore a number of interesting areas. Greif and Zuravin (1989) report that previous studies '...do not auger well for the low-income father's ability to parent his children competently' (p480). Of the 17 father placements studied, Greif and Zuravin's findings were not dissimilar to the previous studies. Fathers tended to be substance abusers, violent towards wives and girlfriends, uncooperative in their dealings with social workers, and undependable in their behaviour towards their children.

It is not insignificant that women appeared to play a major role in how these fathers gained custody. Paternal grandmothers, girlfriends and wives played significant roles in tipping the balance for custody by standing by them and speaking in support of them. They conclude 'Far from presenting the picture of 'the new man' or the involved father of the 1980s that is so popular with the media, these fathers do not appear to offer very much to their children.' (Greif & Zuravin, 1989, p488).

The focus on fathers, in most of the available literature on child sexual abuse, usually considers the personal characteristics, behaviour and attitudes of the sexually abusing ones. Almost no studies include consideration of non-abusing fathers; one that does suggests that are many similarities in the two (abusing and non-abusing groups). Ash (1984) argues that the characteristics found in abusing fathers are also to be found in the non-abusing population as well. Violent and tyrannical, domineering and sadistic, ineffective and pathetic are some of the characteristics suggested. Ash goes on to outline some of the findings of the Hite survey of 7,239 men, which '....illustrates how the meeting of emotional needs and the identification of those needs, is so often in sexual terms...'(Hite, 1981, in Ash, 1984, p47)

The position of men and of fathers in research, and more generally in society, may have some influence on how they are regarded by professionals. This regard will no doubt also be influenced by the roles men and women undertake in society, particularly in the 'caring' professions. Finkelhor (1991) suggested that as the position of women in society has strengthened, the status of the professions and roles they have fulfilled may rise in the future, and more men may be willing to step into these roles and professions. 'It has not been the major revolution that some predicted a few years back, but there are some encouraging indications, and this will have positive implications for child welfare.' (Finkelhor, 1991, p20). While Finkelhor's optimism is laudable, he does not provide us with any evidence to support the notion that there will be 'positive implications' for children and their welfare (see Pringle, 1992).

Gomes-Schwartz et al (1990), in their study of 156 sexually abused children and their families, did acknowledge fathers, and admitted the difficulties in assessing their relevance. They were only able to collect data on fathers from 30% of the cases studied due to their unavailability or unwillingness to participate, and concede that any interpretations from such results would be inappropriate. My own attempts to research mothers and fathers met with very similar difficulties. Our deficiency (as researchers) in approaching and involving fathers must be addressed, as we cannot expect workers to be successful where we have failed.

A main aim of this chapter has been to highlight the imbalances in the literature about parents and child sexual abuse, and how prevailing opinions influence further research and practice. The almost total invisibility or absence of non-abusing fathers is an issue which researchers need to address. Society is now acknowledging that fathers exist, and public policies and attitudes are shifting, the opportunity must not be missed.

# 4

# Missing fathers

I HAVE already pointed out that I was not successful in my attempts to interview equal numbers of fathers and mothers; I either failed to reach non-abusing fathers, or they did not volunteer to be interviewed. On the whole the sexually abused children in this study did not have non-abusing fathers (or did not have access to them), and the non-abusing mothers did not have male partners. Of the seven mothers I interviewed, only one (Mary) was in regular contact with the father of the child, and although two (Jane and Edith) had male partners who were in the role of 'father', none of these men were willing to be interviewed. It became clear, in the brief discussions the mothers and I had about the possibilities of the fathers being interviewed, that there were a number of different ideas about what 'fathering' might involve.

Over the last fifteen years or so attention has increasingly been drawn to fathers' roles; men, women and children have ever increasing and differing expectations of what fathers should be. Quite often these expectations conflict, and images and ideologies arising from the dilemmas can be increasingly frivolous.

*Daddydom is big stuff lately, and it seems to be everywhere—in books, in movies, on TV, and just a teensy bit on some people's nerves. (Sackett, 1988 p18).*

An opposite view of the position of fathers has been nearly as common. The *Sunday Times* editorial (21.2.93) blamed the absence of fathers for the '... uncontrollable behaviour of today's sink-estate male teenagers.' Conversely, Campbell (1993) argues that in homes and communities where there are large numbers of men unemployed, fathers (and uncles and sons and brothers) are all too present. 'The social space men inhabit becomes solely local and domestic .... In unemployment, men's flight from fatherhood has no hiding place.' (Campbell 1993 p202).

The role of fathers whose children are in danger or in pain, however, is far from frivolous and, not surprisingly, is far from frequently discussed or over exposed. In fact, the serious study of fathers and fathering generally is very much in its infancy, and a great deal more work needs to be done (Richman & Goldthorpe, 1978; Lamb, 1981; Backett, 1982, McKee & O'Brien; 1982, Coltrane, 1988, Sachdev, 1991; Hawkins and Dollahite, 1997).

There are conflicting interpretations about the position of fathers in recent history. According to Lowe (1982) fathers' rights over their legitimate children have substantially declined, and are now in more or less equal position with mothers legally. This is in sharp contrast to the position argued by Collier (1995) who points out that an 'equality model' of heterosexual relationships between men and women is flawed. Collier states that "parents do not come before the law as ungendered bearers of abstracted legal rights; they are beings subjectively committed to identities ... within which they might find themselves both powerful and powerless" (Collier, 1995, p191). This was certainly apposite in Susan's case: despite evidence to the contrary (Golombok and Tasker, 1997), she found that her identity as a lesbian rendered her powerless in the child protection arena.

Coolsen (1993) offers a contrasting picture of fathers today and suggests that recent figures (relating to the United States) show that 'more than half of the children born now will spend some or all of their childhood in a family without a father in residence [and of non-resident fathers] ..... the majority see their children only several times a year.' Garbarino adds: 'in some communities, fatherhood is an anachronism'. (1993, p 52). Of the small sample of children in this book, less than a quarter had regular access to a non-abusing father. While it is clear that only a proportion of the children here had access to a non-abusing father or father-figure, it is not clear (except in Julie's case, when father – Jack – was the parent I interviewed) what sort of role was taken by the men.

It is possible that the role of the father is changing, or that the interpretation of 'fathering' is changing (Palkovitz, 1997), but the direction of these changes is not clear. One study of rural fathers found that while attitudes toward fatherhood had changed, behaviour had not (Kennedy, 1989), and similarly, a study of middle-class couples living in Scotland found that fathers were more involved but still peripheral to the family (Backett, 1982). According to Palm and Palkovitz (1988), fatherhood is in a state

*Availability of fathers*

|  | mother | n-a father available | mother's male partner available | father\abuser |
|---|---|---|---|---|
| Jason | Jane | x | ✓ | x |
| Dana | Alice | x | x | ✓ |
| Matthew | Susan | x | x | x |
| Luke | Susan | x | x | ✓ |
| Ann | Astrid | x | x | x |
| Caroline | Mary | ✓ | ✓ | x |
| David | Sally | x | x | x |
| Ben | Sally | x | x | x |
| Darren | Edith | ✓ | x | x |
| Julie | (Jack) | ✓ | ✓ | x |
| 10 | 9 | 3 | 2 | 2 |

of flux, and according to others is expanding (Dienhart & Daly, 1997) and developing (Hawkins et al, 1995), but Segal (1990) concluded that there was little convincing evidence of any change in the amount of practical child care men actually do. Segal wrote of 'the myth of the good father', and is one of the few academics who considered child abuse in her discussion of fathers.

> It is a cause for great concern that the new stress on fatherhood can be exploited to bolster the harmful (if, as immigrant British know, frequently hypocritical) pro-family rhetoric of the right.... The idea that women today receive more help from their male partners is very convenient as this government returns the full burdens of care to women in the home. (Segal, 1990 p54).

# Images and ideologies of fatherhood

It is difficult to study the notion of fatherhood without an evaluation of the concept of patriarchy, as the two terms are often used interchangeably, and confusion around images and ideologies relating to them are not uncommon. Remy (1990) laments the confusion in meaning and propounds that the word 'androcracy' avoids ambiguities and may therefore be preferable.

However Remy's definitions and distinctions between patriarchy and fratriarchy (p44) may be of greater relevance to studies of fathers and men in that they distinguish between two types of oppression. On the one hand patriarchy is a paternalistic, moralistic and somewhat antiquated style of domination; fratriarchy is a younger, self-interested and 'wilder' form of power. It may be that the more rigorous and prescriptive child protection procedures might signal a change in style for the child protection agencies from patriarchal to fratriarchal. Sally described the professional response to her concerns about her four and eight year old sons:

*I had the police at me door. They wanted to take my two sons away without me, to interview them on a video-tape.' (Sally).*

As men are seen to be important to children as symbols of power and authority (Fein, 1978), it might be useful to retain both concepts of patriarchy and fratriarchy when discussing fathers and considering their relationships within families and in society. It is important to note, however, that only one of the children referred to in this book chose to tell their father about their abuse (although four out of ten children had access to non-abusing fathers or father-figures). The symbolic power and authority of men which is supposedly important to children, seems not to extend to it being useful in protecting the children here, at least in their own estimation. Mothers and step-mothers were told first by all but one of the children. (Disclosures will be discussed further in chapter seven).

The literature broadly seems to suggest that although some men have become more active in parenting, their numbers still remain small (compared with those male parents who are still only minimally involved in a parenting role) (Franklin, 1984). Various proposals have been made as to why most men continue to play only a small part in parenting (Lummis, 1982; Coltrane, 1988), but the argument that men gain a power advantage in society by not participating in childrearing processes is convincing (Polatnik, 1973-74; Hanmer, 1990).

## Father-child relationships and experiences

A number of authors have attempted to predict fathers' roles and relationships with their children (Grossman, Pollack & Golding, 1988; Danziger & Radin, 1990; Cox et al, 1992). Psychological characteristics, particularly their autonomy and job satisfaction, predicted the play time and quality of interactions of fathers with their children (Grossman, Pollack & Golding, 1988). Mothers' autonomy was also an important factor in predicting fathers' caretaking and weekday time involvement, as was mothers' job and age (Grossman, Pollack & Golding, 1988). These researchers concluded that men's fathering is strongly affected by their 'wives', and viewed fathers as integral, individual components of a larger interpersonal system—'a complex, multilevel relational family system' (Grossman, Pollack & Golding, 1988, p90).

Franklin (1984) suggests that as more research is being focused on men's' role as fathers, more is being discovered about their child-care activities. He says that sex-role orientation, education and sex of child (among other things), all 'seem to influence the fathering role' (p114). He does not describe the relationship or the tasks involved in fathering and it is not clear what any increased involvement might consist of. He refers to a study by Booth and Edwards (1980) which suggests that fathers spend more time with their child(ren) than mothers if the child(ren) are daughters and if the couple have a relationship where 'one parent dominated' (p113). Without examining the nature of the involvement, or addressing the gender\power imbalances in families, no meaningful conclusions, as to the roles of fathers, can be made. How much do fathers contribute to the rearing of their children and how are their relationships with their children effected by this? McKee (1982) points out that traditional social survey methods of providing answers to such questions are flawed, and her case-study approach revealed a number of interesting observations.

She discovered that although the fathers in her study expressed the importance of their sharing the care of their babies with their partners, there was a wide variation in what this actually meant. In some cases it meant that fathers took on more domestic tasks (eg general housework) rather than any direct physical care of their child. For the majority of fathers 'sharing' did not mean a fifty\fifty division of the tasks, and their involvement (or lack of involvement) depended on a variety of factors, practical and psychological, and increased or decreased over time.

Along with other writers, Chodorow (1978) emphasises that although daughters 'turn to the father' as part of their psychological development, they remain strongly attached to their mothers, and fathers never become so emotionally dominant. The typically late and insubstantial role they actually play in a child's life may mean they are the target of much idealization and, as Eichenbaum and Orbach (1982) suggest, bitterness. Many writers who study fathers fail to consider emotional issues, and almost all disregard child abuse entirely. Lisak, in a piece about fathers and sexual aggression (Lisak 1991), does not appear to have considered child abuse in his analysis; for many boys, their first close encounter with an adult man may be abusive. All but one (Darren) of the boys referred to in this book had very little contact with non-abusing men prior to their own abuse (and all but one of them (David) were abused by adult men).

Only one of the boys (Luke) was abused by his father, but if, as Lisak suggests, the role of father is not just important to sons for physical and emotional closeness, but is crucial to providing 'an opportunity to internalise 'masculinity', not merely imitate it' (p257), then Luke will clearly face extra difficulties. The theories that link paternal deprivation, insecure masculine identification and violent behaviour are compelling (and might be even more so if they included child abuse), but Lisak argues that it is society's reliance on the gender divide that perpetuates sexual aggressive behaviour in men, rather than father-distant child-rearing.

It appears that whatever the extent of their involvement, father's do appear to influence their children and Lamb (1986) emphasises that this influence could be beneficial or harmful to a child's development. Morrison (1991) provides detail of his positive experiences with his daughter, and his relationship with her is carefully considered. This account bears many similarities to those given by mothers (eg Grabrucker 1988) and confirms, as do the parents in this book, that there may be more similarities than differences between fathers' and mothers' relationships with their children, and that these relationships can be positive.

## Fathers as a focus for study

Academic interest in men and masculinity is a recent phenomenon, although a great deal of research and theory has always been designed, conducted and developed by men (and often contained men—studies of crime and delinquency, employment and unemployment, and so on).

However since the 1950s with the strengthening of feminism and the growth of gay scholarship, sociological and psychological work as well as literary and historical studies have increased, and Men's Studies are now established at colleges and universities across Europe and the USA (Hearn & Morgan, 1990). According to Brod (1987) a basic tenet in men's studies is that certain types of biases characterize research on men in topical areas not consistent with traditional male role expectations. Cook (1988) explores these issues in some detail in her study of fathers whose children have died of cancer, and their implications for practice are important. She points out:

> ... the bias we must be alert to is not the tendency to view the masculine as generic ... but ... an implicit female bias ... through the use of female-centred standards and criteria.' (Cook 1988 p286)

Research and theories relating to families has shifted focus during this time too. According to McKee and O'Brien (1982) from the mid sixties to the early eighties fatherhood became a substantive issue and '... mother-focused research programmes have become increasingly out-moded and criticized'. (p3). They suggest that most of the research in Britain has focused on the transition to fatherhood, the relationship between fathers and infants, and the experiences of fatherhood in single and remarried families.

On the whole research has presented men as alternative mothers and much has been done to 'prove' they are as adequate or as desirable parents as mothers. There has been little research undertaken other than looking at the behaviours of fathers compared with the behaviours of mothers with their children, and even less focused on children or fathers with special difficulties or needs.

Both Hearn & Morgan (1990) and McKee & O'Brien (1982) speculate about the reasons for the increased interest in men and fathers and are alert to the possibility that it could represent a backlash against women and mothers. Men, facing competition from women outside the home, are attempting to compete and appropriate the domestic domain in which women were previously autonomous. Whether this theory or others predominate, it is widely accepted that the tendency towards mother-centred family and child-care\development studies in the past has led to poorly formulated research and an uncritical and patchy body of knowledge on fathers.

## Fathers and child sexual abuse

Strand, in her introduction to a study of treatment with mothers in incest families (1991), laments the little attention given by researchers and practitioners to mothers '..by and large the victim and perpetrator have received far more attention.' (Strand, 1991, p377). While it is likely that she is not wrong in this observation, she fails to also note the lack of attention paid to non-abusing fathers (partly because her study, and so many others, focus on incest and fathers as perpetrators).

Myer's study of 43 mothers (of daughters who had experienced sexual abuse by their fathers or father surrogates), contributes to the perpetuation of an over-eagerness a) to examine mothers and neglect fathers and b) to portray fathers as perpetrators (Myer, 1984). The focus (at one point in her analysis) is on the mothers' relationships with their own mothers (despite the historical questionnaire apparently seeking information about both parents). The only information we are given about the fathers (of the mothers) is whether they sexually abused them.

Recent data about the prevalence of child sexual abuse suggest that while some fathers do sexually abuse their children, this may not be as habitually as the literature propounds (Finkelhor et al, 1990). The study undertaken by Finkelhor and his colleagues, interviewed a sample of 2,626 American adult women and men by telephone about histories of sexual abuse. Only 6% of girl victims and no boy victims reported abuse by a father or step-father.

Some problems with methodology in relation to this national survey were acknowledged (connected with the imprecision of the screening questions), and it was accepted that rates may have been higher than reported as some respondents may not have considered their experiences to be abusive, and therefore not reported them. It may also have been an underestimate on the grounds that the closer the relationship the more reluctant a victim is to reveal abuse (La Fontaine, 1990).

What is not acknowledged in Finkelhor's study is one of the long-term effects of sexual abuse in childhood which is amnesia. Maltz and Holman (1986) suggest that as many as 50% of all survivors cannot remember their abuse experiences, and it seems likely (though, as yet, not explored sufficiently in the literature), that the 'greater' the trauma (including the greater the betrayal), the greater the likelihood of dissociation and memory-loss (Fraser, 1987). It is also likely that the study by Finkelhor and his colleagues, like all other self-reporting studies, under-represented the prevalence of child sexual abuse generally, and particularly under-represented the younger child's experiences, the experiences of children who were not able to speak (and possibly more likely to be victimised), and the most traumatised and betrayed children.

Clearly it is not possible to identify accurately how many fathers abuse their children, and equivalently, how many do not. It must also not be forgotten that many men (and as has been stated elsewhere, prevalence studies reflect some uniformity in identifying the vast majority of abusers as men), may be fathers who abuse children other than their own—grandfathers, for example ( see Margolin, 1992). However it is scarcely credible that all fathers of sexually abused children are abusers.

Why does the literature regard fathers of sexually abused children as either guilty or irrelevant\absent?

## Agencies' responses to fathers

Agencies' responses to fathers are often inadequate. Greif and Bailey (1992) question whether social workers really understand fathers. One of the conclusions of Stevenson and her colleagues (Stephanie Fox Review Panel, 1990) that a lack of 'systematic attention' to Mr Fox (Stephanie's father) and to his family history, attitudes and personality may have contributed to a poor risk assessment and a failure to protect.

Jack felt that the agencies were neglecting him and his family at one stage.

*We just made the decisions. We were starting to worry and panic when nobody seemed to be going to come around. As I say we got several explanations and some of them seemed half genuine as to different social workers, and leave, which obviously I know things has been cut back and cut back, but at the end of the day my priority was Julie, I wasn't interested in too many excuses. (Jack)*

Agencies tend to expect paternal absence and have been negligent by failing to develop approaches that might increase fathers' involvement with their children (O'Hagan, 1997; Trotter, 1997; Milner, 1994). Similar findings have been reported in the United States (partly inspired by the growing cost of welfare being mostly associated with father-absent families), a program was developed especially to increase fathers' involvement in Head Start (Levine, 1993).

Levine suggested that a number of issues needed rethinking if policies were to be developed successfully. Firstly he advocated a new framework for thinking about father involvement which acknowledged the participation of fathers in their children's lives, however small, or whether formal or informal in nature. Secondly encouragement should be focussed on the quality of the relationships rather than the quantity, and lastly the 'social context' of the involvement should be acknowledged and addressed (how relatives, staff and others feel and react to father-involvement).

Levine's emphasis on 'quality' is an interesting one and poses additional dilemmas for agencies developing a less gender biased response to fathers. While it may be convenient for many professionals to support over-stretched fathers (and mothers) in the belief that quality is more important than quantity in time spent with children, this is probably an over-simplification. Palm and Palkovitz (1988) point out that an undefined minimum amount of time is needed before children are receptive; they may have basic needs to be met. '... parents who can afford to invest great quantities of time with their children are more likely to share quality time with them when it is appropriate.' (Palm and Palkovitz, 1988, p361). Even in families where fathers are at home a lot (through unemployment or ill-health for example), we have seen that they are still considerably less likely to participate in child-care than are mothers. Professionals '... tend to implicitly express a bias that mothers are primary care-givers and fathers assistant parents by stressing the (as yet unsubstantiated) assertion that mothers 'allow' fathers to participate in caregiving, and that fathers learn parenting skills by observing mothers'. (Palm and Palkovitz, 1988, p369).

Professionals must not only be aware of the different attitudes and expectations faced by fathers, they must also be prepared to do something about their difficulties. By failing to address the problems, professionals and their agencies are frequently guilty of compounding them.

## Conclusion

It is likely that the gaps in the literature regarding fathers of sexually abused children is part of the overall absence of specific data on fathers. Research, like practice, has tended to focus on mothers, particularly when dealing with emotive issues (eg illness, abuse or death), even when claiming or intending to work with or study 'parents'. There may be a number of reasons for the relative lack of attention given to fathers in research and practice, but practical issues seem to be the major cause for mothers being involved, as they are more frequently available and more easily accessible (by virtue of their being the most likely carer) than fathers.

The recruitment rates of mothers and fathers for this book do not bear out this simple reasoning however. Although only one father came forward (compared to seven mothers), my letter of information did not specify the custody status or relationship of the mothers and fathers I was seeking. It is likely that there were many factors contributing to the small numbers of volunteers of both sexes, and it is possible that the networks that were best able to help mothers and fathers were those linked to survivors groups, which are predominantly female.

A number of the women I met through this book had male friends and partners who were fathers of children who had been abused, and it is likely that one or two of them would have received my information. However, at the time of the interview only Jane and Mary had male partners who were in father\father-figure relationships with the children, and neither of these fathers were able to take part. The fathers' experiences with professionals during the course of investigations and protection planning may or may not have been influential in their reluctance to talk to me.

It is clear that professionals need to rethink their approaches to working with fathers. Social work in particular, has failed to involve fathers with its services (see Marsh, 1991), and the effects of the relatively new concepts of 'parental responsibility' and 'partnership' in the Children Act are continuing to be measured. It will be interesting to see what the next decade will bring.

# 5

# The reactions of mothers and fathers

I HAD a number of ideas as to what a mother or father's reactions might be, to learning that their child has been abused. I had expected some extreme anger and demands for retribution, and I had thought that some mothers and fathers might be overwhelmed by their emotions. I was not prepared for the diversity of reactions and responses. Feelings ranged from despair to relief and subsequent responses were both considered and instinctual. Reactions not only varied between individuals but also changed over time, and were recollected and reported differently. Some were considered to be constructive and positive reactions and others were perceived as negative and harmful.

Manion and his colleagues (1996), in a study of 63 mothers and 30 fathers (of children who had been sexually abused by someone outside the family), found their reactions to be profoundly effected by 'secondary traumatization' resulting in feelings of self-blame, loss and helplessness. They found that mothers were traumatised by the discovery or disclosure of sexual abuse, and the severity of distress was related to their own perceptions of themselves as parents, rather than to any variables about the abuse (Manion et al, 1996). These, and other researchers, make it clear that parents' reactions vary widely and are related to a great deal of differing factors (Byerly, 1985; MacFarlane, 1986; Hooper, 1992; Booth & Booth, 1994).

There may be some danger in generalising too much about reactions, as subsequent responses may become narrow and restricted. There is also a tendency for people to blame the parents rather than the perpetrator for the sexual abuse and the child's distress, which compounds and complicates parents' reactions (Ehrensaft, 1992; Wattam & Woodward, 1996). 'We, and our children, are not monsters or incompetent. We are like you normal... We are being punished for the rest of our lives, our children are no longer innocent... It is the offender who should be punished.' (Wattam & Woodward, 1996, p121-2).

It must be remembered that each situation is unique and needs to be dealt with as such. The reactions of the mothers and father I spoke to were varied, but there were a number of reactions that were shared and commonalities existed around anger particularly, but also about guilt and denial.

## Anger

I had expected that Jack might express more anger than some of the mothers, and other authors have assumed the same (Regehr 1990), but this stereotypical and sexist assumption was wrong. The mothers expressed a great deal of anger. Mary described how long-lasting and diffuse anger can be, as well as how intense.

*.... we were absolutely gobsmacked to put it mildly and so angry at everything. We were furious with him. My partner's reaction was he wanted to go out and kill him. .... we still have a lot of anger in us. (Mary)*

In the work undertaken with mothers at The Children's Hospital in Dublin (Staunton and Darling, 1992), much of the early stages '...were characterised by intense and angry feelings towards the perpetrator of the abuse.' The mothers reported that two of the most valuable things they learnt from the group sessions were a) that 'feelings of anger, fear, resentment and shock were all normal', and b) how to manage their anger.

All of the parents involved in this book expressed anger in one form or another.

*I just didn't know what to do, I was just devastated you know....ah......I didn't know whether to smash everything in the house or kick the doors or just scream - WHY?, WHY?....With everything he's had to put up with, why Jason?' (Jane)*

Susan in particular felt that her anger was often beyond her control, which she found frightening.

*I've got one hell of a temper. There are times when I can't control it. (does that frighten you as well?) Yes. I've hit two or three people. I've hit my son, I've hit my girlfriend. There was a time I didn't know I'd* hit her. It's all happened in the last 4 years, I've got really screwed up. I've had brain scans and everything. They're treating me for epilepsy. (what do you think it is?) *I think it's just sheer bloody temper, but I've tried to tell them that but sometimes I can't get out, you know, I go down, just pass out. (Susan)*

Alice also was confused about the cause of her anger and was not sure whether it related to the abuse of her daughter or to her own abuse.

*Dana got sexy to me which made me very angry. Eric had raped me - this was like Dana raping me too. (why did you get angry?) The last night my husband spent in this house he raped me. So, I know this might sound stupid this but, Dana making advances to me was like him making advances to me, he's done it to her and then she's doing it to me. (Alice)*

Similarly for Susan who had been sexually abused by her brother when she was a child herself.

*When he was 13 I put him into care because I'd hurt him. I just went berserk one night and took my temper out on him, where I should have took it out on my brother. (did he remind you of your brother?) Yes, a walking double. The more I see him the more I want to throw up. (Susan)*

Byerly suggests that many mothers feel repulsion for the offender, and that this may trigger physical reactions such as nausea, as Jane did.

*I felt as if I was going to explode inside, I felt sick. (Jane)*

MacFarlane (1986) predicts that many parents will feel rage and an urge for retaliation. She advises parents not to react on impulse or seek to settle the score as this would add to the child's distress. Burgess et al (1984) reported parents showing strong feelings of anger and rage. 'One father was observed at a hospital, while his son was being examined, beating the walls with his fists' (p121). It is not unusual for mothers to express their rage in similarly violent ways.

*.... I wasn't going to sit back and let that happen. I just totally went raging. Every time he hit my son I hit him back. I did exactly what*

*he did to my son, I did it to him. It got to the stage where I couldn't handle the fact that I was doing it to him. I was getting really......really taking power on. He was a softy, he never lifted his hand to us. I think it's sheer bloody temper and frustration and anger because I can't express how I feel, and I tend to hit out. (Susan)*

Hooper (1992) points out that mothers may also have to deal with anger directed at themselves; many children express feelings of anger to their mothers for 'failing' to protect them from abuse. Similarly mothers and fathers may have to face anger and hostility from other family members for 'causing trouble', for involving 'outsiders', or again, for 'failing' to protect. Jack, Jane and Susan experienced a great deal of such antagonism and bitterness.

On the whole the anger expressed was specific and triggered by a particular incident or directed at a particular person or object. Byerly says that mothers are angry at someone specific - at their child for 'doing this', at the offender for violating the child and\or betraying her (the mother\wife\partner), at themselves for not protecting their children. (Byerly, 1985, p11). She adds that some mothers are also angry at the workers involved in the investigation\protection\treatment. Jane experienced this in relation to her son's abuser.

*.... where I realised we were sitting in the same room as the bugger who'd done it to him. He was 17 or 18 now so it was pretty scary. I wanted to kill him you know but I restrained myself. As I left the court I had to pass the lad, standing with his solicitor, I don't know how I didn't strangle him. I got down the stairs and burst into tears.... I got a phone call that afternoon from the Social Services saying I'd have to go back to court because I'd upset the lad. They said they'd had to get the clerk to get me out. I said that's a load of shit, I was angry but I didn't make a fuss, I kept my voice down. I was furious. (Jane)*

Jane's experience may be a good example of when anger can be a healthy response, one which is channelled into pursuing justice and supporting the child. Susan's anger however was less discriminate.

*What I would love to do is to castrate all the men, well not all men, I'd love to castrate all the bad men. That's what I feel like doing. I'd castrate my husband, but I didn't get the chance.* (why not kill them?) *Yeah, get a gun and shoot them. You know this society really stinks. I'd like to get all the child abusers in a great big field and drop a bomb on them, and blow the buggers up. (Susan)*

Byerly (1985) notices a similar experience 'many mothers feel angry at everyone around them, a kind of general anger'. Mary, in a different way to Jane, was also able to manage or channel her anger in a constructive way.

*... in my imagination I've done all sorts of horrendous things to him, and none of them are terrible enough in my opinion for what he's done. Realistically though I've got this tremendous .. I don't know whether it's anger .. or angry energy, but I decided it would only serve to frustrate me to have this anger in me. So what I'm trying to do is use this in a positive way. (Mary)*

# Denial

Similarly to the angry reactions, denials differed in strength, duration and focus. Not all of the mothers denied the reality of the abuse, but many of their families and friends disclaimed or rejected it to some extent or other.

*Immediately all that side of the family just took his side and totally rejected my daughter, and said she was just lying and made it all up.* (what about Nana's son [Caroline's father]?) *Well he believed her, and I believed her straight away, my partner believed her straight away, her dad believed her, my mother believed her, my sister believed her, but none of them would even ever come and find out why. (Mary)*

According to Berliner (1991) family members, like the sexually abused child, may avoid imagining or thinking about what actually happened to reduce their own painful feelings. 'Unfortunately this may lead to a lack of empathy for the child's experience and reinforce avoidance as a primary coping strategy'. (Berliner, 1991, p36). Berliner lists examples of barriers to belief: a parental history of abuse, which they promised would not happen to their child; a belief that they must terminate a relationship with an abuser once abuse is confirmed; excessive dependence on the abuser; or prior family rejection of the abuser, resulting in a situation where to believe is to accept family condemnation.

Women's responses to their own experiences of sexual violence include 'forgetting' and minimizing (Kelly, 1988). It is not surprising therefore, given the dilemmas involved and the threats to their well-being and livelihood that discovery involves, that some mothers may not actively pursue such information in relation to their children. According to Hooper (1989) '..such responses are better understood as coping strategies than as collusion.... (p25). Susan, who was sexually abused as a child, had some difficulties initially with accepting the abuse, but it is not clear (and she is not clear herself) whether her own childhood experiences affected this.

> *Then things went really, really bad. My son started coming out with things like his dad had been trying to put his willy up his bum, and things like that. At the time I didn't want to believe him because I knew my son didn't like him and I thought ah well he's just saying that. (Susan)*

Byerly (1985) says mothers often experience disbelief and denial. Addressing mothers directly she says 'You may keep asking yourself and others if this is real, is this really happening, how this could be possible, if you are dreaming'. She goes on 'You may not believe your child, especially if the offender says he never did any of the things she is accusing him of. You may resist information and evidence'. (p11) Byerly does not emphasise that information and evidence often conflicts, and does not clearly advise mothers how to select the 'right' information. Susan, at this time, had evidence which suggested that Matthew was jealous of her new husband and wanted him to leave.

> *...I didn't believe him for the simple fact at the time he hated my husband because he was so jealous. (Susan)*

'It is our contention that learning to work effectively with mothers who do not, or cannot, believe that their children have been sexually abused, is the biggest and most critical challenge facing workers.' (Craig et al, 1989, p72) Of course the phenomenally greater challenge might be learning to work with fathers, but that is not yet being considered.

Craig and her colleagues (1989) suggest that workers who deal with mothers who do not believe that abuse has occurred, face feelings of helplessness, despair and frustration, yet must go on to assess why the mothers are unable to do this. They do concede that its the perpetrators and not the mothers who are responsible, and add that the issue to address, therefore, is not so much one of 'failing to protect' but one of establishing the expectations of mothers as responsible parents (Craig et al, 1989, p73).

In their experience where mothers have problematic relationships with their children (including emotional or physical distance) and a lack of 'what are viewed as maternal protective behaviours' (p73), they are less likely to believe that abuse has taken place. This is even greater when there is a strong emotional tie between the mother and the perpetrator. Craig et al (1989) go on to recommend the involvement of resources in the community, especially other mothers who have been through similar experiences. However they suggest this is only necessary 'where formal treatment offers are not taken up (p73).

In her very practical book for professionals Faller (1990) explores the motivations of the 'non-offending' parent to lie, at the time of disclosure. She admits that although the non-offending parent is more likely than the abuser to acknowledge the abuse (and respond appropriately), 'she' may also '....deny, disbelieve, or discount the allegation, especially in interfamilial sexual abuse cases'. (Faller, 1990, p117) She goes on to list the dynamics which may influence a non-abusing parent: acknowledgement of shortcomings as parent; acknowledgement of shortcomings as spouse; decision re leaving or staying with abuser; facing practical consequences of that decision; coping with professionals' intrusions. She concludes that these dynamics '.....usually result in....a reluctance to believe by the non-offending parent.' (Faller, 1990, p118). Faller, like Byerly, fails to acknowledge the existence of contradictory information and evidence.

Byerly (1985) points to an experience of 'numbness' which mothers report; this inability to feel anything (emotional or physical) at all, which may be linked to shock, may add to a mother's difficulties around believing.

For too long I had been pushing my suspicions to the back of my mind. I wasn't able to accept that he would do anything like that to her.....Even though I thought I was ready to hear the truth, I was deeply shocked.' (Driver & Droisen, 1989, p70).

Denial, as such, may be only for a fleeting moment, or may be suspended instinctually, as Jack experienced.

*My whole, my whole system just fell apart. I could not even ... I had no comprehension of what had just happened. I was the one who had asked Julie to take Michael upstairs and I ... I just ... I couldn't ... So instincts took over. (Jack)*

Researchers and practitioners alike need to remember that reactions to traumas may be transitory, and like Jack's, operating from an instant and instinctual response rather than a measured cognitive process. Both reactions may be appropriate or inappropriate, and mothers and fathers may experience both types of reaction. Practitioners should not be surprised then if changes, particularly relating to denials, take place, and they should certainly allow some time for these shifts to occur.

*It was actually the school that turned round and said your son's been abused. I can't remember the teacher, they said it to me over the phone. I says no. So I went down and it was the doctor who said bend him over and .... he had been interfered with in the back end and I never ever knew. I was so angry. I went looking for my husband ... I had a knife. (Susan)*

Susan's immediate reaction appears to have been denial, but she went to the school and quite quickly changed her position. She may have been less inclined to deny the abuse if the information had been presented to her in a different way, or by someone else.

*There was never any doubt. I don't think she would ever have lied about that, she was so consistent, so there wasn't any problem with that. (Mary)*

*My daughter told me when she was looking at some old photos of her grandfather. She said 'dirty old man'. I believed her immediately because he'd abused me. (Astrid)*

For two very different reasons Mary and Astrid were able to believe immediately that the abuse had taken place. Unfortunately both reasons can be contentious for other children and their families. Older children (and Mary's daughter Caroline was 14 year old) are more able to give consistent accounts of abuse than infants are, and mothers' own experiences of abuse as children is often taken as evidence of their own unreliability by practitioners (as mentioned earlier in this chapter). Both of these points will be discussed further in chapter six.

## Guilt

Jack felt remorse because it was his 'side' of the family who had abused Julie, and ideas about abusing or 'dangerous' families (as opposed to individuals) may not have helped him. When investigating interfamilial abuse practitioners need to be clear about their suspicions regarding possible perpetrators.

*I felt pretty guilty because its all my lot. (Jack)*

    McFarlane (1986) addresses parents (of children who've been extrafamiliarly abused) directly, advising them that guilt or self-blame are useless emotions and there was probably nothing they could have done to prevent it happening (p300). She goes on to advise parents to control their feelings. 'You may be screaming inside, but you must make every effort to be calm with your child. It may be the hardest role you've ever had to play - and the most important. (p304) Such advice might also be helpful for non-abusing parents in interfamilial abuse cases, but it must be remembered that children need (and deserve) authentic and honest responses from the adults who are caring for them, so 'role-playing' may not be of use.
    Hooper found that several mothers in her study reflected an ideology of selfless motherhood, even though their own responses to their child's sexual abuse had rarely been straightforward. '....this concept of selfless motherhood represented a major source of conflict and guilt.' (Hooper, 1989, p26). Fathers do not escape feelings of guilt either.

*It was about 6 weeks after this that we initially found out. It was a social worker called Susan that took over, and what started to become apparent was that this wasn't the only incident. This is where I find probably, you know, this is where the real pain starts for Dana and I. The fact that Julie had been carrying things for about two years. (Jack)*

It is not always clear as to what the guilty feelings are relating to, and Alice felt guilty about her dreams, and about not being able to express her distress.

*I even, not so long ago, dreamt that I saw Eric sexually abusing Dana. He turned to me and laughed at me, and she lay there enjoying every minute of it. I felt so guilty about dreaming such a thing ..... obviously its in my mind all the time.*

*I've not really cried yet - I've kept it down, thinking of her and not myself. Perhaps I should have released my feelings. It's like telling a story - not like it really happened to me. I feel guilty for not crying. Can't settle at night - nightmares, screaming, bottling up ... and I feel guilty because I'm not crying. (Alice)*

Jane found it hard not to feel responsible as she believed her son Jason felt she was guilty.

*Jason got out of the surgery fine but when we got home he just went to pieces. Crying and crying, then he got angry, I didn't know what he was going to do, I thought he was going to kill someone. It was all my fault for making him go there. He just looked at me - a terrible look.... he threw himself over his bed, shaking and screaming. Sally was crying and crying you know, she was just a baby. I thought I've had it, I can't cope. (Jane)*

Byerly (1985) says that most mothers feel guilt and self-blame, and that these feelings may be overwhelming at times. She says that mothers may blame themselves for a number of things, including not knowing about the incest. Jane felt guilty for being angry with the professionals.

*Looking back I feel very guilty for what I did to them, but I just felt so angry at all these people who did nothing. At the time I felt they didn't know what they were doing. (Jane)*

Susan still feels some guilt about her own abuse.

*I keep punishing myself for something that isn't my fault, I haven't learnt to accept that yet, and I don't think I will until the actual court case. I just find it so hard to cope with all my feelings. I was abused five times, including my mother. (Susan)*

## Loss

Edith experienced loss at a number of levels. She had lost her child (almost literally as he nearly died on more than one occasion), and had lost control of him as a mother.

*During the last twelve months he's slashed his arms with knives, bits of glass, his current phase is tattoos.... He'll be up, he'll be tipping the tables over, and punching the walls. Usually I jump on his back, if I think he's going to hurt himself. I hang round his neck. He carries me round like a rag doll, but he comes out of it then. (Edith)*

Hooper felt that Breakwell's concept of 'threatened identity' (Breakwell, 1986; Hooper, 1989) was useful in relation to the mothers she studied. This analysis is concerned with loss of self, loss of roles (eg of mother or wife\partner), loss of ideas about the future (for themselves or for the family). Hooper identified a number of these and other issues in relation to the mothers she interviewed. Feelings of inadequacy and guilt were common, sometimes in relation to their 'failure' to prevent\protect, and sometimes at their inability to 'make it better' as mothers so often can with childhood injuries. Inadequacy, frustration and ongoing distress were all emotions expressed by the mothers and father in this book.

## Pain, Anguish and Grief

Mothers and fathers described an extensive range of other feelings which they experienced at different times. Within hours of discovery or disclosure of the abuse, for example, some devastating experiences were shared by both fathers and mothers.

*And then my wife and I were sitting here, Julie crying. What to do, what shall we do? We just had no idea. It was a bombshell. (Jack)*

*Now I remember when she was about three years old (and we were visiting), she told me he'd touched her when she was sitting on his lap. I was numb, ... sick, .... paralysed. ... couldn't say anything. (Astrid)*

A number of authors refer to some individual psychological distress for family members associated with disclosure of the victim's experience. 'Parents may have secondary post-traumatic symptoms or depression or may relive prior unresolved abuse trauma.' (Berliner, 1991, p38-39). MacFarlane (1986) acknowledges that a parents' memories of childhood trauma may be rekindled by the disclosure of their own child, and suggests that parents need therapeutic help in dealing with this. However, Finkelhor (1984) found that the one group of parents who did significantly better than others in talking to their children about sexual abuse were the parents who had themselves been victims. Both Astrid and Jane found this to be the case in the longer term, although initially Jane found her memories were getting in the way of her helping Jason.

*I was just.......I just did not know what to do. He told us on the Wednesday and by Friday I was just demented, absolutely demented. I'd begun to get pictures of what had happened to me because I vaguely remember being abused. I remember my step- dad doing something to me and I'd told my teachers but nobody believed me when I was young..... I was really having to push back my memories to take care of Jason. (Jane)*

Sleep disturbances due to worry and distress were common, as Jane and Alice described.

*I couldn't sleep or anything, I ended up ironing all night. When Pete came down in the morning he didn't know what to say. I didn't know whether I was coming or going, I was just crying, crying, crying. (Jane)*

*I'm frightened to release my feelings. .... I've had a lot of nightmares, a lot of dreams and restless nights. Its all bottling up and I can't settle on a night-time. Fear of being trapped and screaming in the middle of the night for help. Dana's found me and wanted to know if I was all right. Maybe I'm frightened to release all my feelings bottled inside. (Alice)*

Other psychological difficulties were experienced by Susan.

*I took an overdose three months ago, I really wanted to kill myself. They had us rushed into hospital and put us into coronary care. The ones I took were for my fits. I take fits and I'm violent and I don't*

## The Reactions of Mother and Fathers

*know what I'm doing. (Susan)*

Alice found it difficult to express her feelings.

*Every Christmas that comes round now...there's that there about it. This was the time...God, it was a terrible Christmas. (Alice)*

Susan and Mary expressed shame or embarrassment, and not just for themselves.

*They asked us about the marks on his neck and I said he got them when he was playing outside because I felt so embarrassed about my husband doing it. (Susan)*

*(what were you ashamed of?) That I'd failed, I'd failed as a parent and I hadn't protected her. The major priority in my life is to love the children and to give them the best care that I can and I failed .... I looked upon myself as a failure. Perhaps I'm trying to make a recompense for that. (Mary)*

Jack and all the mothers felt they had let their children down in some way, and that others compounded this in various ways.

*Children who've been sexually abused are like pushed to the side, people are scared of them. All things like this really hurt me. (Alice)*

*The experiences he's had he's not a child. He can never be a child now. He's been in the drug circles with the drug dealers and all sorts, I mean. I can never make him be 14 again. (Edith)*

*It's a situation which has been a nightmare in some respects. It's like road traffic accidents - they're just statistics unless you're directly involved, or you know somebody. We found ourselves in water, we didn't know how deep it was, we didn't know how to get out of it. With reflection, it was by accident that we got sorted out, if that's the right word. (Jack)*

Jane felt that the professionals had let her down.

*I had a very, very raw deal from the person who was supposed to be helping me, the social worker, very, very bad. The psychologist left. (Jane)*

Craig et al (1989) emphasised the need for professionals to give mothers a therapeutic opportunity to deal with their feelings, and liken these to a grief process (especially the 'denial stage'). They also talk of professionals' feelings (see chapter five).

Sgroi and Dana (1982) identified a number of feelings experienced by mothers at the time of disclosure, including inability to trust, poor self-esteem, limited social skills and depression. However, Wagner (1991), in a study of 104 mothers, found that mothers who seek psychological services for their sexually abused children exhibit no higher level of depressive symptoms than do mothers seeking help for their non-abused children. This result is interesting for a number of reasons: 1) it might be expected that mothers of sexually abused children would be more depressed than other mothers; 2) it might be expected that children of depressed mothers would be more vulnerable to sexual abuse than other children.

Jack and Susan (and some of the others) wondered whether their feelings or concerns about other issues may have distracted them from what was going on (and no doubt compounded their feelings of guilt too).

*There had been attempts, incidents, up at me mothers. We were so wound up with Peter and this business with me mother, we possibly, possibly may have missed some of the signs. We think that Julie may have probably took the view that we had enough on our plate. We don't know. (Jack)*

*I gave my son up to live with his grandma and his father, and that was the biggest mistake I ever did. At the time I couldn't cope with my own feelings and ... all my problems .... I feel really upset and hurt, what's happened to my two children. (Susan)*

A word that was used a lot by the mothers was 'hurt', and Susan and Mary use it repeatedly when describing the pain and distress they felt.

*(how did you feel when you found out about your sons?) I was really hurt about it because I was hurt myself by abuse and then having to see my son upset about it ... (Susan)*

*... although the abuse didn't happen to me, it did happen to me because someone did that to my child ... that really hurts and that makes me really angry. (Mary)*

Byerly (1985) says mothers often feel hurt and betrayed by the abuser (as well as their child) in cases of incest. They may even feel that the abuse took place deliberately to hurt them. Similarly Byerly says that mothers often feel jealous of the sexual relationships their partners have had with their children. According to Hooper (1989), when the perpetrator was the mother's partner, feelings of rejection, threatened sense of sexuality or femininity, and betrayal of trust were also experienced.

Susan felt betrayed by her family.

*It was the same with my youngest son. He was three, no five, and I got a call off my mother-in-law, telling us I hadn't to worry that my son was passing blood from his back end. So I went back to Social Services and told them. I had to wait with my mother-in-law, and I was an imbecile because she kept saying I turned everything round. (Susan)*

Edith felt that her family shared her loyalty and resisted betraying Darren.

*But at the end of the day the younger children don't want their brother sent away. I certainly don't want him sent away, I think he's got enough to contend with and I think he's got to have the support from home. Even though he's doing things he knows are wrong, but in time he's going to come to terms with it. (Edith)*

## Acceptance

One of the most difficult things for the mothers and father to do was to accept not only that the abuse had happened, but also that they had not prevented it or protected their child. It was often also difficult for them to persuade other relatives that the abuse had happened, as Jack found.

*I said you're not going to hear this, or you're not going to take this unless you hear it direct from Julie .... So I just asked Julie to go in the kitchen with my mother and just say what happened in simple words. And she did. And my mother came out and said, well the bairn cannot be telling lies. (Jack)*

Accepting their child's view of things was also difficult, this was particularly so for Alice whose daughter Dana made up nice memories of her father.

*I don't like it. I think he's a horrible person, he was a horrible person when I left him, and I didn't even like being married to him, but I have to accept it for Dana's sake. I've got to accept the way that she feels. I've never pulled him down in front of her. (Alice)*

In a study undertaken by Myer in 1984 it was found that mothers (of daughters who had experienced sexual abuse by their fathers or father surrogates) experienced a succession of reactions to hearing about the incest. These were not unlike the experiences reported in grieving a death; denial, guilt, depression, anger, and finally acceptance.

Hooper (1989) however, argues that the analogy with bereavement, similar to De Yong's analogy with rape (1988), has limitations. Sexual abuse, unlike death (or rape), is not a clearly defined event with an end, but 'one which tends to have on-going and unpredictable ramifications for years and years.' (Hooper 1989 p23). For the mothers in her study, the discovery process was rarely straightforward and often chaotic, involving for some suspicions, confrontation and denial, conflict over the meaning of behaviour, self-doubt, and sometimes uncertainty over who the abuser was.

The experiences of the mothers and father in this book were similarly far from straightforward, and their acceptance of the different bits of information was gradual and difficult. Realizing that they may have 'missed' vital clues and signs for long periods of time, was particularly hard, especially for Jack.

*The most stressful, or most painful thing for me was that Julie couldn't come to us, or chose not to come at the time. The fact that she actually carried it. I could still get upset now if I focused my mind on that. (Jack)*

'Facing the memories' is what Byerly describes as a stage of discovery when a mother (and presumably a father) can expect to piece together 'all the clues of past months or years... or all the messages you were given by your child or her\his offender that you never heard'. (p17) It is likely that mothers and fathers may reflect and consider many incidents and feelings from the past which now hold significance in relation to the sexual abuse, but previously did not. Byerly found that the resulting feelings could reach overwhelming proportions.

> One mother recounted her reactions after her son told her about being molested by her husband (his stepfather). She said that she began to agonise through the memories of husband and son eyeing each other across a room or spending long unexplained hours together into the nights. The same trust and love for them that had allowed her to transcend suspicion also, later, made the incest almost unbearable to face. (Byerly, 1985, p8)

## Longer-term reactions

Memories are only one of the longer-term reactions faced by parents. In a study of family reaction to homicide in the United States Burgess (1975) identified a two-phased syndrome of experience, a crisis phase and a long-term reorganisation phase. In the second phase there is a double impact, 'Families have to deal with their own psychological reactions and they have to deal with the socio-legal issues involved with the crime of homicide' (p395).

According to Burgess, psychological issues include grief work, dreams and nightmares, phobic reactions, identification with tragedy and role change; socio-legal issues are around the concept of blame and the court process. Burgess, who has worked extensively in the field of sex crimes and child sexual abuse, alerts her readers to the need for professionals to be ready to offer help and counselling to the families of other reported crimes.

Hooper found in her work with fifteen mothers that a longer term understanding and intervention would have more relevance. 'The degree to which a mother can regain control of her own life may be limited by factors such as the child's reactions later, other children wanting contact with the father (if he is the abuser) even if she and the abused child do not, and the response of the extended family.' (Hooper, 1989, p23).

Alice continued to worry about her daughter's safety in unrelated areas.

> *I was nearly in tears today driving home worrying if I had an accident and Dana was left all alone. I can get really upset thinking of the fear of losing her. One night I spent the whole night worrying about her choking on a bit of bubbly and me not finding it. I worry*

*a lot about her safety. (Alice)*

Ham (1985) addresses the issue of forgiveness which, he says, is part of the Judeo-Christian heritage, and may be of particular difficulty for mothers (and presumably for fathers too) who have religious beliefs and loyalties. Cashman (1993) considers these difficulties to centre around a more superficial kind of forgiveness based on a Christian duty, rather than on reality, resulting in the Church unwittingly colluding with abusers (p80). Cashman also refers to the Christian emphasis on peace and compassion (p107), which can lead to an unhelpful suppression of anger and rage. Mary felt unable to advise Caroline's father about this, when his murderous desires conflicted with his Christian beliefs.

*He kept saying he's a Christian, and he found it very hard to come to terms with the fact that he actually felt capable of killing somebody, but he genuinely felt that this is what this man deserved. (Mary)*

Staunton and Darling (1992) report that mothers, in the final stage of their programme of group work, were able to gain new confidence and rehearse new ways of responding in order to prevent further abuse to their children. The mothers and father in this book had similarly learnt a great deal about child sexual abuse and about dealing with the repercussions. Alice and Mary continue to develop their expertise in this area, and Jane has become a consultant and trainer who is widely respected amongst parents and professionals.

*I've done a lot of reading about child sexual abuse and I echoed a lot of those stages; anger, guilt (at not having recognised what was going on), and other similarities. (Mary)*

Astrid realised she had learnt a great deal through reading and through thinking about and discussing her own abuse, and was able to respond in a more assertive and positive way to the sexual abuse of her daughter.

*(why were your reactions to her disclosure so different twenty years ago and recently?) Yes. I'd always known I'd been abused (although only recently started making connections and working through the memories), but twenty years ago I was there in the house where it happened to me, whereas recently I was here in my home, miles away. Then I didn't know what I know now - about him being*

to blame. *(Astrid)*

In the longer-term most of the mothers and the father had become 'experts' about managing the after-effects of child sexual abuse, including managing some very difficult behaviour. Edith had especially difficult decisions to make.

*I mean he was at the ..... unit for four days and they did actually have to restrain him when I went through. I had already discussed it before then, because Darren kept saying he was coming home, and I actually told him before he went, I said, Darren, I cannot have you back home the way you are. Because I don't know how to cope with you. I'm frightened in case you hurt the younger ones when you go in one of these violent moods. (Edith)*

Other parents also devised strategies for managing and protecting siblings. Mary (and her partner) and Edith talked to their other children.

*We've got eleven year old twins as well, and we had to ... try and explain to them. We just said their grandfather had done some bad things to Caroline, like touching her in inappropriate places while she'd been staying there; had he ever said anything or touched them in any way that they felt uncomfortable about? Obviously the effect that this has had on all of us has been to make us very sad and very angry, and we've had to make allowances for the eldest one. When she's angry she's not really angry with us, she's angry about what's happened.* (How did you then explain to your other children why Caroline had slashed her wrists?) *It was just that she was in a lot of pain, she was very sad.* (Who gave you advice about what to say?) *Well by this time I'd been raiding the local library, and there was the group. (Mary)*

*I don't think he would ever ....I know the statistics are against it because I've had that drummed into me. I had that drummed into me when he was nine years old - that ... he would go on to abuse other children, that's why I want the help for him now, because I couldn't cope with that. I have spoken to the younger children about sexual abuse, not so much to the five year old, because she's a bit young to understand, not yet, but more to the ten year old and the eight year old. (Edith)*

All of those whom I interviewed had found their own answers

and solutions by involving themselves, in various ways, with other mothers and fathers and with adult survivors. They all expressed a greater ability to respond to their children after having met and listened to survivors. This was not a strategy I found referred to in any of the literature, which may reflect the relatively recent growth in the survivors' 'movement', but may suggest a professional reluctance to acknowledge the expertise found amongst these women.

There are a number of other reactions which have not emerged from the literature, yet were eminently obvious amongst the mothers and father in this book. Courage, tenacity, enterprise and empathy were found in all of them. All of them expressed love, respect and pride in their children who they constantly acknowledged as 'brave' and 'wonderful'.

*Again it was very traumatic, going through the statement, although having said that they, the policeman and the social worker who came were very nice and very kind, tried to put her at her ease; but obviously it was so humiliating for her, and such an effort. (Mary)*

Mary also found first aid useful when Caroline cut her wrists.

*Obviously I was concerned that there was all this blood, but I knew they were like superficial. By then I'd recognised the symptoms and I only wish I had known about them earlier on. (Mary)*

Jane became adept at self-control.

*When he came out with that I was just ah.......I can't describe how I felt....ah.....I just really had to listen to it. I just had to keep a very tight hold of myself. (Jane)*

Susan has become an advocate for Luke, who she believes is still being abused by his father, and for his step-sister.

*I mean I haven't let it lie. Every so often I tell someone. I just feel why should he get away with it? He's just sitting back. He's got a daughter now and he could be interfering with her. It's just totally sick. It's really, really sick. (Susan)*

Some of the skills that the mothers and father developed were clearly excellent. Jane and Mary described their reactions on two occasions, that were only moments in the overall picture, yet were of immense importance to them, and no doubt for Jason and Caroline too.

*I was able to tell Jason that I really did believe him, and I promised we'd get him some help. He said that I couldn't take it away ...... I had to sit and hold him all the time just like a little kid. (Jane)*

*I'll sit on the bed and have a cup of hot chocolate with her or something before we go to bed. Its nice that we're a lot closer, it's getting that way. It's hard work, but she's worth the effort. (Mary)*

It is clear from these accounts that the mothers' and father's reactions were similar in many ways. Their tenacity and strength in circumstances of great distress, seem immense. However, in many ways their trials were compounded by the reactions and responses of the professionals they came into contact with; the child protection 'experts' were not always as helpful as they might have been.

# 6
# The professionals

MAJOR EFFORTS to respond to child abuse since the mid-1970s have focused on a need to establish and develop inter-professional arrangements and mechanisms. The involvement of practitioners from a wide variety of backgrounds and agencies in child protection has increased also, and multi-disciplinary practice and training has been established throughout the country.

Failures in inter-agency co-operation and poor inter-professional understanding have been a feature of more recent concerns (London Borough of Greenwich, 1987; Butler-Sloss, 1989; Birchall, 1995; Hallett, 1995), although they have been problematic for years (Stevenson, 1989). According to Parton, what is needed is that practitioners '... roles, responsibilities and interrelationships, together with their areas of expertise, should be clarified, developed and formalised.' (Parton, 1991, p116)

Whilst Parton's exploration of the balances in co-ordination and management of the different professionals and agencies is informative, it is clear that there remains some gaps in the discussion.

## Professional Attitudes

Prior to the Jasmine Beckford Inquiry (London Borough of Brent, 1985), professionals, and social workers in particular, approached their work with a 'rule of optimism' and made the most favourable interpretation possible of the actions of parents. This attitude was criticised soundly in the Beckford report and appears to have been influential in shaping different attitudes among practitioners. Susan's experiences, however, seem to suggest that the professionals preferred to rely on the more favourable interpretation of her husband's actions towards their son, than on her own.

*The last three years I've tried to do something about it but they keep dismissing me. They keep saying nothing has happened. But I know something has happened. (Susan)*

Professionals' attitudes towards mothers, as well as towards other adults (both colleagues and clients), are as varied as they are problematic. 'Social Workers are generally a fairly good mirror of the attitudes of our society.....Black, working class or single mothers are going to find themselves treated differently and find it harder to fight for their rights once they are caught up in the system.' (Celia Atherton, quoted in Dibblin, 1987, p16). Of course, professionals have also to deal with the prejudices of their clients too. For example Milner (1992) finds that relatives, like professionals, feel mothers are responsible for failing to protect their children.

Paul Stubbs has highlighted some of the problems around professional attitudes when working with black families. He suggests that as black communities tend to have somewhat negative experiences of policing, they are less likely to want to disclose\report sexual abuse, and less likely to expect a good service from them. '...a worrying picture emerges of sexual abuse being used as little more than a pretext for coercive intervention against a community already defined in negative terms.' (Stubbs, 1989, p103). He goes on to say that social workers are similarly placed, with racial stereotypes and racist beliefs impeding their interventions.

Professionals' attitudes regarding sexual abuse may be even more diverse (as are those of the general population), and seem to be highly influential in the service they are able to offer. Doughty and Schneider (1987) argue that workers' attitudes about incest are critical to effective involvement of family members in treatment. In a study of 106 undergraduates, graduates and MA clinicians, attribution of blame decreases as a function of more education, and 'the blame scores of men were significantly higher than those of women on all factors except offender'. (Doughty and Schneider, 1987, p1157).

The researchers conclude that education in psychology and experience in mental health influence attitudes about incest. They go on to add that not only theoretical knowledge, but also actual experience with incestuous families may add to a more complete understanding of the complexities and decrease the tendency to blame any one individual or factor. Incredulously, they do not explore in any depth, (despite discovering an 'unexpectedly high' percentage of subjects reporting a history of sexual abuse), the possibility that personal experience may also increase understanding (Cox, 1993).

Attitudes about the family and the role of mothers and fathers also influence practitioners. Their knowledge of the research in relation to sexual abuse (particularly intra-familial sexual abuse) often seems similarly biased. 'Prevailing negative ideas and attitudes about mothers of girls who have been sexually abused have been yet another means by which society....... have reinforced oppressive family systems that deny the rights of women and children in many families. Social workers have a responsibility to rid themselves of these stereotypes, and challenge them whenever they appear in the course of their work with families where father-daughter incest has occurred.' (Myer, 1984, p57).

Patton (1991) suggests that professional attitudes have shifted over the last decade or so as multi-disciplinary work has developed. However, although professionals can reach high levels of consensus on criteria or indicators for substantiating reports of sexual abuse, it is not clear how much research support exists for many of the criteria agreed upon.

Some of the mothers in this book felt very much alone in their dealings with their child's difficult behaviour, something that professionals should be particularly aware of (Coohey 1996). On more than one occasion, when they asked for help or advice they were told they would manage, as though there was some 'natural instinct' for this. Alice was reassured by her social worker in the most vague and unhelpful way.

*I didn't know how to handle the medical, how to cope with Dana. I asked for advice but was told 'you're a good parent, you'll do alright'. How could I tell her why\ how going to hospital, she already had a fear of hospitals. (Alice)*

The advice Jane received was also unhelpful.

*I thought I've had it , I can't cope. So I rang the doctor and asked to be put straight through. I said look I don't know what to do, what do I do? She said well he's very angry, just let him go. (Jane)*

Jack similarly felt abandoned by professionals and hoped he

## The Professionals

and his partner Diana helped Julie.

*With reflection, I'm not sure still that there's anything set up to try ... I mean, I think the Social Services and the teachers and the case conference thought we were good ordinary people, sensible people, so they just presumed ..., obviously we did our best, but we didn't know if we were doing right or wrong. We learnt by our mistakes and we got on the best way we could. Some of it was not all to do with Julie, but obviously it was all inter-linked. (Jack)*

The final advice given to Alice by her social worker was not only unhelpful, but potentially damaging and certainly far beyond what both Dana and Alice were able to do at that time.

*The social worker's last words to me were to just let her forget about it. I felt like a ten year old being given a baby to look after. (Alice)*

Levitt and her colleagues (1991) have found that primary care-givers (mothers, fathers and other relatives) of sexually abused children reported that there 'was not enough follow-up or action' (Levitt et al, 1991, p50), something which Alice, Jane and Mary very clearly agreed with.

*Professionals were not there enough. They only came on the days they had to come. I would have liked a visit once a week right at the time when it was all happening, just for them to call and say 'are you all right Alice?' (Alice)*

*After the initial interviews and the caution ... that was the end of the Social Services involvement, that was the end of the Police involvement. We just felt that we were left in this sudden vacuum, with all this trauma and nobody to talk to. That really hurt. It was so new, we were so raw. We didn't know who to turn to for help, other than for each other. (Mary)*

*... went straight to Doctor who ... promised to get him some help ... Eventually got an appointment with a child specialist - some kind of therapist ... overall there wasn't much improvement ... Things just seemed to fizzle out then. We went on the same for three years. (Jane)*

The work undertaken by Levitt and her colleagues (1991) suggests that primary caregivers valued highly professionals who were respectful, and established trust and rapport with the victim and family. Jane felt she wouldn't be believed.

*I didn't know where to go or what to do. I had some knowledge of counselling but I just couldn't function. I thought of ringing the police but they'd just say it was a long time ago or not believe us. I didn't know what the hell to do. (Jane)*

Susan felt completely unable to trust the police, not only because they failed to respect her or her convictions, but also because she believed they were corrupt.

*I've tried, I've been to the police for help. To me, my husband's father had paid the police - you know - given them a back hander, to keep it quiet so it wouldn't go against him because his father had a good job, and his mam had a job. (Susan)*

Levitt and her colleagues also report that service providers who 'displayed expertise and professionalism' (Levitt et al 1991, p50), were well regarded. Poor attitudes were also reported, and among those criticised by care-givers were personnel who showed insensitivity to victim and family needs, and those whose behaviour was reported as 'harsh, traumatizing or unethical'. (Levitt et al, 1991, p50). Care-givers also reported that some workers 'displayed negative attitudes or disbelief of victims'. (Levitt et al, 1991, p51)

Pugh and De'Ath (1984) find that many parents felt their confidence was undermined by professional 'expertise', and argue that workers should re-examine their roles and question the nature of their relationships. They advise professionals to value and build on the abilities, the skills and the knowledge that parents bring to their role.

Social workers' knowledge, or acknowledgement of, the strengths of families is ... sometimes tenuous ... they appear to be blind to the 'good side' of family relationships which parents are more ready to identify. (Packman 1989a p89)

Packman goes on to discuss the even more crucial difference in views about the appropriateness of admission to care as an answer to family problems. She reminds us that studies have shown that while social workers tend to want to avoid care 'at all costs', parents, and sometimes older children see the option less negatively. It is unfortunate that Packman does not refer to child abuse at this stage in her discussion, as this surely complicates still further the tendency for parents and social workers to be at 'cross purposes', with the children potentially left out altogether.

Work undertaken by the Clermont Child Protection Unit (Pattison, 1991\92), suggests the importance for work undertaken with victims of child sexual abuse and the non-abusing members of their family, to be closely co-ordinated with the assessment and treatment of the perpetrators. On the face of it this seems to be an excellent suggestion which most mothers and fathers would welcome; it may help them and their child to understand events and to clarify issues. However, Pattison argues '..that both pieces of work need to happen in tandem ... if there is to be any possibility of the level of risk of further abuse in such families being reduced to an acceptable level' (Pattison, 1991\92, p16). They appear to assume that without this families would not be able to prevent risk of further abuse (whatever the definition of an 'acceptable' risk might be).

Despite acknowledging that 'the non-abusing parent, (usually the mother)' is the strongest ally to the unit, Pattison and her colleagues suggest that they could only find dominated, weak, unaware, and unsupportive mothers with which to work. The workers found that most mothers were unable to believe what they were being told for quite a long time, and when they eventually did do, their reactions of feeling guilty and\or responsible were unhelpful to the professionals in their work with the perpetrator.

The work of Pattison and her colleagues at the Clermont Child Protection Unit is disappointing. Their inability to value the mothers' feelings and experiences, or to support them collectively, surely contributed to their presentation as 'weak and dominated' individuals. Hooper (1989) points out that '....substituting powerlessness for collusion does not provide an adequate understanding of the range and complexity of mothers' responses. The debate has sometimes taken the form of whether mothers are co-perpetrators or co-victims, defining women only in terms of their relationships with either partners or children.' (Hooper, 1989, p22). Hooper goes on to emphasise that it is important for workers not to assume that because powerlessness is an issue in common for women and children in a patriarchal society, that they are both equal in their powerlessness nor that they necessarily have interests in common.

Nor should it be assumed that powerlessness is static, non-abusing mothers and fathers' positions can be changed, but professionals seem reluctant to take any power from the perpetrators, let alone share it with dis-empowered parents. These very negative attitudes on the part of professionals appear to be common in the literature and in practice, and quite often stem from some simple errors of thinking:

1. failure to distinguish between fathers, step-fathers and father-figures, and between them and perpetrators;
2. failure to acknowledge the different levels of awareness, ability, and understanding that all humans have in relation to child sexual abuse, and that professionals will be at different points on such a continuum alongside non-abusing mothers and fathers;
3. eagerness to assume that there is only one non-abusing parent;
4. eagerness to assume that incest offenders only commit sexual offences within the family.

Where professionals are able to acknowledge some strengths in families, they tend not to look beyond female relatives, and often only consider mothers. 'It is generally the mothers who must become more alert and sensitive in defence of their children' (Staunton and Darling 1992). The authors do not explain why it is mothers who must do this, nor why fathers might be excluded from the responsibility of defending their children from sexual abuse, but it may well be linked to institutional perceptions of women as 'problem-bearers' (Butler & Willott, 1993, p346).

## Myths and Stereotypes

There are a large number of myths around child sexual abuse, and the majority of these focus on women\mothers and girls\victims. Many of these have been developed around stereotypes of incestuous families, on which much of the early research and writing focussed. While it is important not to deny that some women\mothers do share the blame in the abuse of their children (and some women\mothers do abuse), it is mostly men who abuse ((Finkelhor, 1986) and most mothers who try (and succeed) to protect (Hooper, 1992).

For a number of reasons however (Trotter, 1993), a whole collection of myths surround mothers which function to reinforce their culpability in the abuse of their children. Amongst these is the myth that mothers rarely intercede to protect their children from sexual abuse and frequently collude with or shield the perpetrator. this forms the main plank of the 'family dysfunction' or 'systems' models (Furniss, 1991). Worse still, Lustig (1966) stated 'We were impressed with [the fathers'] psychological passivity in the transactions leading to incest. The mother appeared the cornerstone in the pathological family system'. (Lustig, 1966, quoted in Driver & Droisen, 1989, p36). This distorted interpretation of a situation was the least likely scenario amongst the mothers I interviewed.

*I kept repeating over and over that I would never leave him or stop loving him and that he wasn't dirty .....Obviously, by this time I was crying as well, so I just cuddled him and told him I loved him, and that what had happened to him wasn't fair. Jason said he'll kill me now and you'll hate me. I said I won't, I won't, I'm here and I'm staying with you. It took me till about two in the morning to calm him down. (Jane)*

Taylor(1993), outlining what he sees as the 'feminist challenge' to this element of the family dysfunction model, locates the family as 'a place where women and children are at risk of being abused by men', (Taylor, 1993, p140). This emphasis on gender relations and power imbalance is central to the feminist critique of professional collusion with abusive situations and provides a crucial focus for all professionals in this area. Other researchers have found that most mothers were supportive of their children, whether or not they knew the perpetrator. 'No statistically significant differences could be found amongst the three maternal response groups [ie supportive (without emotional changes), supportive (with emotional changes), or non-supportive of her children] and the relationship of the perpetrator to the victim.' (De Jong, 1988, p18), yet Lustig's interpretation prevails among many professionals.

One common thread amongst the myths around mothers is that they are to blame - by being absent (by illness, work, death or sexual withdrawal etc); by reversing roles with their daughters; by being passive, masochistic and\or dependant; or by having particular personalities.

Friedrich (1991) suggests that studies of the personalities of mothers of sexually abused children would help us understand how sexual abuse could occur and be sustained over long periods, although he is cautious not to link 'maternal pathology to a blanket conclusion of maternal duplicity'. Similarly, the myth that mothers frequently encourage (consciously or unconsciously) incestuous relationships between father and daughter, is common. 'The prevailing point of view in the literature is that mothers of incest victims typically respond poorly when confronted with allegations that their children are being abused.' (Gomes-Schwartz et al, 1990 p110). The myth that mothers fail to support\protect their children because they are unable to make good relationships with them (or anyone) due to their own poor relationship with their mother, is a more recent one to emerge. Workers may often be unaware that their thinking and planning is based on myths, and probably assume that reliable research findings are behind their assessments. For example Staunton and Darling (1992) write 'In the second stage, mothers were beginning to make links between their experiences and their families of origin and their present situation which may have allowed the abuse to occur.

Many practitioners are correctly aware of some links regarding abuse and different generations in families, but fail to locate responsibility for the abuse with the perpetrator (and possibly his family of origin) instead focusing on the situation and mothers' responsibility for that situation having arisen. However, it must be acknowledged that in the evaluation of the work by Staunton and Darling, this new understanding (ie of how the family of origin has affected the present) was one of the three most valuable things the mothers themselves felt they had learnt. Perhaps there is a tendency for professionals to perpetuate myths intergenerationally: blaming mothers, and their mothers' before them!

It might be useful for researchers and practitioners in future, to focus their work on the families of origin of non-abusing fathers, and on how their abilities (or inabilities) to form relationships have influenced their abilities to protect their own children. In comparing fathers with mothers in this way, a more realistic picture may emerge. Strand (1991) suggests that the tendency to blame mothers occurred because mothers had been judged against unrealistic standards. 'The subsequent, inevitable devaluation of them when they do not live up to the idealized image accounts for the blame attributed to the mother.' (Strand 1991 p379).

There are a number of myths prevailing that may be applied to fathers as well as mothers. One of these is their failure to support\protect their children because they are immature and unable to take responsibility for their actions. Stereotyping can also lead to misperceptions about fathers (Barker 1994), about men who were sexually abused as children (Mendel 1995), and about men generally (Cavanagh & Cree, 1996).

According to Byerly (1985) mothers need to have their feelings listened to and respected, 'to be cared about and not taken for granted by children, friends, people in 'the system'.' (p16) It is not surprising that as procedures swing into action mothers and fathers may feel out of control; decisions are swiftly taken out of their hands and their emotional vulnerability may be mistakenly construed as 'immaturity' or even inadequacy. The atmosphere of suspicion, which often extends beyond the period of investigation, compounds the feelings of impotence (Cleaver & Freeman, 1995). According to Byerly mothers want to regain control, not only of their lives, but also of their minds. 'Most women say they need to .... recover their identity'. (p16)

Another myth that may be applied to either parent is that they fail to support\protect their children because they have many ungratified emotional needs of their own and therefore turn to their children for nurturance. Whilst this is true of many parents to some extent, it does not appear to be a prevailing cause of child sexual abuse, indeed distant relationships (particularly between mothers and children) seem to correlate higher with sexual abuse (Finkelhor, 1986, p74). Yet the notion of emotionally immature and unsupportive mothers endures. There has been little effort amongst researchers or practitioners to differentiate subsets of mothers and there is little data available about the ways in which mothers differ from this stereotype (Gomes-Schwartz et al 1990).

There are a number of conflicting myths around child sexual abuse in different generations of the same families. Firstly it is believed by some that mothers and\or fathers are fearful and over-protective of their own children because they were abused themselves as children.

> (... you said a number of times that you talked to Social Services). *They just totally dismissed us, they just turned round and said just because you were abused it doesn't mean your children are. (Susan)*

Conversely, it is believed by others that mothers and\or fathers fail to support\protect their children because they were abused themselves as children and cannot bear to remember\consider it again. It is not surprising that conflicting beliefs abound as both positions (and many others) do exist, yet professionals tendency to stereotype mothers and fathers into one group or another, creates myths which prevent good practice. It is as likely (if not more so) that parents who have experienced child abuse in their families of origin will be more likely to be able to support and protect their own children. Mary was clear that her partner Jim was better able to support Caroline because of his own childhood memories of the perpetrator (his step-father).

*(... maybe your husband had incidents in his own childhood which helped him believe her.) Yes ... he must have been about three or four when his mam married this man ... he seemed to make an overt fuss of treating him as his own child, and giving him everything, but when his mam was out he'd lock him in the cupboard under the stairs. So he's had this cruel streak in him perpetuating the abuse. (Mary)*

Myths also surround fathers, often linked to blaming them (as with mothers), although not often for their absence. Fathers are often believed to be unable to be helpful\supportive\decisive because of their tendency to distance themselves from the caring role - particularly in times of acute emotional distress. This did not appear to be the case for Jack.

*Obviously we had a clear path. Our main and overriding priority was Julie. (Jack)*

The other most common myth linked to fathers is that they are unlikely to be able to be helpful\supportive\decisive because they are most likely to be guilty in some way. Recent findings suggest that fathers may not be as guilty as once thought. As discussed earlier (see page 37) a study published in 1990 found that of the girl victims, only 6% (less than 2% of the whole sample of women) were abused by a father or stepfather (Finkelhor et al 1990).

Unlike myths, many stereotypes about child sex offenders and victims have been laid to rest among professionals. That 'dirty old men' prey on unfamiliar children in playgrounds is an outdated notion and research has been responsible for shifting this attitude among practitioners. However many workers still regard perpetrators as stereotypically one type of offender. According to Abel et al (1986) most abusers have had significant experiences of other types of sex offending (up to 10 types);

indeed, they suggest that one-type offending is rare.

The stereotype of the child who often seduces the offender into sexual activity - wittingly or unwittingly - is similarly outdated, although there are professionals and parents who still believe that most children comply because of their own needs for attention\affection. Byerly (1985) for example, points out that mothers commonly ask whether the abuse was their child's fault; this did not seem to occur to the mothers in this book. 'The notion that child sexual abuse typically involves gentle seduction is seriously challenged. Children most often comply with sexual offenders because they are afraid to refuse' (Gomes-Schwartz et al, 1990, p73).

## Discrimination

As discussed earlier, professionals' attitudes are likely to mirror those of society generally, and this would include their prejudices and capacity to discriminate. Black and Asian mothers and fathers, whether they are treated differently to white mothers and fathers or not, are likely to receive unequal services from white workers and predominantly white agencies. Mothers and fathers belonging to other minority groups, such as disabled, lesbian\gay, working class or single parents, are also likely to receive different services than their majority group counterparts (Taylor, 1993; Jackson, 1996; Logan et al, 1996).

Other forms of discrimination also exist. 'Since its inception in 1976, Parents for Children has argued that there are people with special knowledge and skills and great potential as parents who are at present discarded by adoption agencies because of issues in their past' (Walker, 1991). If professionals are willing to make such erroneous decisions about potential adoptive parents, how much more likely are they to apply these prejudicial criteria to the mothers and fathers of sexually abused children?

The mothers and father in this book were aware of the dangers of discrimination, but more often felt that if discrimination would show itself in relation to their children's new 'label' as a victim of child sexual abuse. They often felt themselves to be powerless to help their children or themselves with this dilemma.

*What's Dana going to be like when she's older? I'm frightened she's going to be classed as a tart or a slut. One friend of mine who's just had a baby turned round and said to me, 'I don't want them sleeping over, I'm so frightened Dana's going to touch the baby'. Children who've been sexually abused are like pushed to the side, people are scared of them. All things like this really hurt me. (Alice)*

It is often suggested that lesbian mothers are even less capable than heterosexual mothers of protecting their children from sexual abuse; indeed it is not uncommon to hear that their sexuality may in itself be a form of sexual abuse (Campion, 1995).

*I'd got rid of my husband, and I found I couldn't handle being with the lads so I'd turned gay. Then I got that thrown in my face because I was a queer. So I had arguments with her. The social worker asked if I was sure I hadn't touched my son. I said of course I haven't what do you think I am? Then I explained to her about my being abused by my father, and being raped. I just couldn't handle any more. (Susan)*

According to Byerly (1985) 'Lesbian mothers say that their sexual preference often becomes an issue when incest is disclosed' (p19), and King (1995) suggests that much of the concern is based on the common misconception that paedophilia is somehow linked with homosexuality. The issue may arise when statutory agencies attempt to assess suitability for parenting\protection, or may be used by the offender in attempts to discredit the mother (to her children, to his family, or to the statutory agencies).

Discrimination and prejudice frequently surrounds 'Asian' communities whose mothers are thought less likely to protect their children from sexual abuse than other mothers, as they are prevented by cultural traditions from speaking out against men. Byerly (1985) points out that it might not be unrealistic for mothers whose partners are black, to fear that they may be treated more harshly than white men by predominantly white institutions and agencies. According to Driver & Droisen (1989) black mothers are in a dilemma; they do not want to put their children through racist procedures, yet they want justice for them. The Social Services are often not sympathetic to the quandary that mothers and children experience and many Social Services employees believe that Black families are more likely to abuse their children than white families (Driver & Droisen, 1989).

According to Ahmad (1989) 'For too long the social work profession has tinkered with the welfare of black children and young people, and research portrayed the black family as the 'problem', allowing racist myths, assumptions and methodologies to interfere with their effectiveness.' (Ahmad, 1989, p165). Other racist stereotypes can be equally damaging and untrue. For example, the notion that West-Indian mothers are less likely to protect their children from sexual abuse than other mothers, as their 'happy-go-lucky' nature ensures a minimising of the seriousness of the abuse.

Other difficulties arise for African mothers and fathers in particular as it is often assumed by white professionals that all African cultures endorse 'ritual circumcision' of girls, and that mothers collude with these practices. Professionals often go on to assume that the judgements of these mothers, about all matters relating to children and safety, are therefore unreliable. According to recent statistics (Hedley and Dorkenoo, 1992), less than half the African nations practice female genital mutilation (a more accurate definition of the phenomenon), and many African women leaders and heads of state are actively against the practice.

A semi-official discrimination exists amongst professionals in relation to those who are perceived as 'difficult' individuals. Mothers or fathers who have mental health problems (particularly if displaying 'bizarre' behaviour), are less likely to receive services as Jane found.

> .... the traumas I was suffering meant I got taken into mental hospital. I wasn't allowed to see the children at first, then after I got out I wasn't allowed to take them back to live with me. I realize now that I was just too ill to look after them, but at the time it was terrible. I had a very, very raw deal from the person who was supposed to be helping me, the social worker, very, very bad. The psychologist left. (Jane)

Similarly, where practitioners or their agencies are not prepared in the provisions for people with disabilities, services will be seriously limited. Finally, facilities are often not offered to people who have been violent or who are dependent on drugs or alcohol as both Edith and Susan experienced

> At the moment nobody will give him any counselling because he has a drug problem. Which is very little at the moment, in fact there's no street drugs involved now, its usually pills or tablets he can get off anybody. (Prescribed?) Oh yes, they're prescribed, but not for him. (Edith)

*If I'd got the proper help I wouldn't be in the state I'm in now. (What's proper help?) The social workers never helped. The last time I had him I couldn't control him, he just went totally rage on us. I phoned my mother-in-law, he'd set all the alarms off in the shopping centre, all the alarms in all the shops. I just couldn't ... I just picked the phone up and said you'd better come down, because I will string him up. (Susan)*

## Professional Practice

Professionals rely on a number of sources to inform and improve their practice; reviews, research, traditions, management, inspection reports and training. More recently they have come to rely on the recommendations of Inquiries. The motivations for agencies, and particularly for Local Authorities, to follow these recommendations (and be seen to be following them) are powerful - not least among them is the desire to avoid such inquiries themselves.

The findings and recommendations of inquiries are not always consistent (Department of Health, 1991a) and, according to Parton 'It was as if there were two competing agendas or paradigms for practice' (Parton, 1991 p78); one to be bold, decisive and pro-active and the other to be conservative, careful and quiet. He believed that it was the former paradigm, characterised by the inquiries, which was predominant at the time of the Cleveland cases.

The 'Pindown' report highlighted a number of profiles of children (whose experiences may or may not have involved sexual abuse - this information was not central to the inquiry), which included some association with parents, and in particular, mothers. Whilst the report was unable to provide much detailed information about the involvement of the children's parents (one of it's central criticisms was about inadequate recording), mothers were frequently referred to as being ill, absent, unable to control their child, or generally inadequate. Fathers were also mentioned but less frequently, and often with less information. For example, one entry clearly implies the unsatisfactory morality of a child's mother, but offers no opinion or information about her father, 'Susan's father was one of her mother's subsequent boyfriends' (Levy & Kahan, 1991, para 11.18).

The report goes on to tell us that another mother (in agreement with her daughter) expressed the wish for her discharge from care and to be allowed to live together. Despite these requests not being met, the Inquiry did not feel it necessary to recommend that mothers or fathers be given right to complain. 'We recommend that a complaints procedure for staff, foster parents and children should be implemented without delay, and should contain an independent element.' (Levy & Kahan, 1991, para 23.34)

Levitt and her colleagues (1991) found that primary caregivers (mothers, fathers and other relatives) of sexually abused children valued highly professionals who were supportive, understanding and reassuring. They also reported that service providers who 'worked hard, did a good job and got results' (Levitt et al, 1991, p50), were well regarded. Other qualities which were praised by care-givers were for staying involved throughout the process and helping the victim talk about the abuse. Poor service delivery was also reported and among those criticised by care-givers were personnel who appeared incompetent or inadequately trained, and services which lacked co-ordination or communication between the agencies involved.

Some professionals have been doing excellent work with mothers and fathers for years. Smith and Breathwick (1987) described the work of family resource centre whose workers, for example, were able to help a mother and step-father understand and care for their daughter who had been sexually abused by her father for six years. Voluntary organisations and volunteers have a considerable 'record' of good practice.

'I don't think I could have gone through it all, if it hadn't been for the support of the Incest Survivors' Campaign and Women's Aid. They also helped me to press charges and to get through the eight-month ordeal of the court case. Each time I had to appear in court, women from ISC came with me.' (Sian, in Driver & Droisen, 1989, p71).

All of the mothers and father in this book had some involvement with voluntary agencies and Jane and Mary were active volunteers themselves in individual work, group meetings and training events.

According to all of the mothers and father in this book group settings seem to have been successful for them, in work with adult survivors and non-abusing parents. Whilst group work is a common method for voluntary agencies and self-help associations, it does not appear to be as commonly used by statutory organisations.

In the group work undertaken by Staunton and Darling (1992) mothers described their feelings of frustration and devastation when professionals showed a lack of understanding about child sexual abuse. The mothers felt it would be better if professionals were honest and admitted their lack of 'answers'. In contrast the same mothers reported feeling comfortable with two group leaders who were able to provide information and insight, and control the group.

Mary found, similarly to the mothers in Staunton and Darling's work, that professionals showed a lack of understanding; but unlike those mothers, found that professionals were also too controlling.

*It was too controlled because there was so much emotion in that room - they just left. As they got to the door they just turned round and said 'oh by the way you've got an appointment at the hospital tomorrow for the doctor to examine you and check you're ok'. Well that was a catalyst .... WHOOSH ......, but they were gone then. (Mary).*

Staunton and Darling also point out some of the difficulties in attempting to provide an appropriate and useful service to mothers. They found that therapists often felt de-skilled, and that they needed 'endless patience for slow growth and an ability to recognize small improvements'. (Staunton and Darling 1992). They go on to say that although groups were demanding and often induced feelings of helplessness in the leaders, they suggest it is important not to 'abandon' group members who drop out; they may feel that they are able to return later, or may need to join a new group in the future.

Strand's application (1991) of Finkelhor's model (Finkelhor et al, 1986) of 'traumagenic dynamics' to mothers, helps workers view the mother's position more empathically and '..incorporates the social reality of the discrepancy in power between the mother and her partner and allows the woman's voice to emerge, separate from her role as mother or partner.' (Strand, 1991, p380). Strand suggests that feelings of powerlessness and betrayal are the ones that need to be addressed in the initial phase of 'treatment'. Feelings of powerlessness and betrayal may have been themes in a mother's life and relationships for some time, and may now be compounded by the interventions of various agencies and legal requirements. Strand suggests that workers must be aware of

## The Professionals

these conditions and incorporate them in their response to the mother. (Powerlessness will be discussed further in chapter eight).

Strand goes on to suggest that the middle phase of 'treatment' requires the working through of the feelings of stigmatization and sexual trauma as identified by Finkelhor (1986). The importance of helping mothers to articulate and understand these feelings is emphasised, and the need for workers to be aware of their own attitudes to sexuality as well as the mother's attitudes is stressed.

A major area of difficulty for professionals and non-abusing parents alike is the so-called 'contamination' of evidence or testimony by prolonged therapeutic work (Tate, 1991; Stroh, 1995). This was specifically referred to by a number of mothers and fathers, but might be of even greater significance for children (and their non-abusing parents) who have different communication systems from spoken English (Westcott, 1993).

Berliner (1991) outlined a number of therapeutic targets for work with parents or other family members. These were: increasing family participation in child recovery, promoting relief and support for the victim, addressing the psychological effects of the victim's experiences on other family members, and improving family functioning. 'The evidence suggests that the improvement of a child victim after the abuse is over is substantially related to the family's capacity to contribute to a solution, and that, whenever possible, therapeutic interventions should also include components directed at the family.' (Berliner, 1991 p36). A number of the mothers in this book felt that professionals failed to consider the needs of the wider family, particularly siblings, but Jack felt that the focus of the professionals, if not the timing, on to themselves as a couple (instead of onto Julie as a victim), was useful.

*The second week we went, she [General Practitioner] formed an opinion, and I couldn't disagree with her, that Julie was a super girl and she was responding admirably, but she [[General Practitioner] seemed more concerned about us. To be quite honest I couldn't disagree with her.....she suggested we needed some counselling sessions. So we went for seven or eight hourly sessions, and they were pretty inconvenient, in the sense that getting away from work etc. The first three or four I came out with terrible headaches, it was quite traumatic. But she made us realise that we were split in several directions, and really it was what we wanted. (Jack)*

## Professional Caring

According to Packman (1989a) the numbers of children under five coming into care has fallen dramatically in the last twenty years (30% of admissions compared to over 50%) 'as policy has shifted towards providing planned 'packages' of support and therapeutic\educational programmes for parents with problems'. (Packman 1989a p86). Astrid's difficulties might well have been handled differently if they had happened more recently.

> *I was having psychological problems. She went into care for three years with foster parents. I had her home every week. Initially the arrangement was only for six months but I was still afraid I couldn't cope so I extended it (because if I'd had her back and then failed she might have had to go to new\different foster parents). I was still worried after three years, but was worried too that the foster parents might want to keep her. I was surprised how well I managed. (Astrid)*

Packman goes on to highlight successful ventures in both the statutory and voluntary\self help arenas which may have contributed to these figures. However she does not make it clear whether the 'packages' improve the quality of life for either children or adults, let alone whether they reduce the incidence of abuse (sexual or otherwise).

The help and advice needed by adults who are caring for sexually abused children is acknowledged and documented, though invariably relates to people other than the child's mother or father. (Faller, 1990; Davis, Kidd & Pringle, 1987; McFadden, 1984; McFadden & Ryan, 1991; MacFarlane, 1986). Training programmes for residential care workers, foster carers, adopters, teachers, nursery workers, etc. have all been developed over recent years, and much attention has been given to foster carers in particular.

Faller (1990) states that '...foster parents who care for sexually abused children require special training and guidance so they can address the unique needs of these children.' (p181) She goes on to outline suggested topics for their training:

(1) An exploration of attitudes and feelings about sexuality and sexual abuse
(2) Normal childhood gender identification and sexual development
(3) Normal adolescent gender identification and sexual development

(4) Sexual sequelae of sexual abuse
(5) Behavioural sequelae of sexual abuse
(6) Strategies for management of sexual sequelae
(7) Strategies for management of behavioural sequelae
(8) Variations in victim attitudes and emotional reactions to the sexual abuse, the mother, and the offender
(9) The causes of sexual abuse
(10) Variations in the reactions of non-abusive parents to sexual abuse
(11) The dynamics of relationships between sexually abused and non-abused siblings
(12) How to handle visitation with the sexually abusive family.
(Faller, 1990 p181-2).

Whilst not denying the need for such work, it is disappointing that most authors do not see the need or application of such ideas to mothers or fathers. Do they not deserve such training (despite their children being 'unique'), or is it that they could not benefit from it? The Department of Health (1989b) suggests that 'appropriate training should be provided for carers' (p14) and seems to include parents in their interpretation of 'carers'.

Davis et al (1987) provide an excellent documentation of a seemingly thorough training programme in child sexual abuse for foster carers with teenage placements. As well as initial and on-going training, carers were provided with individual and group support as it was felt the tasks undertaken by carers were 'demanding....and require great skill and perseverance.' (pii) Presumably the tasks when undertaken by a potentially distraught and distressed mother or father are even more demanding and require even greater skills and perseverance. It is astonishing that professionals have generally not extended these ideas about support and training to non-abusing mothers and fathers.

Some notable exceptions can be made here. Kee MacFarlane provides a sensitive and useful beginning to such considerations, although she confines herself to helping parents cope with extrafamilial molestation (1986). Richardson and Bacon (1991) emphasise the importance of supporting and helping mothers who subsequently were better able to act more supportively towards the child and with less hostility to professionals. They go on, 'We ignore the needs and strengths of mothers at our peril: they are the child's best resource and without them, children can only have a second best chance to overcome the effects of sexual abuse' (p144). Griggs and Boldi (1995) outline a treatment program for parents of 'abuse reactive' children, which, although including the children, emphasises the fundamental part played by parents.

Jack felt it was fortunate that he (and Diana's) needs were not ignored by professionals, as he felt that his abilities to look after his immediate family had been depleted.

*at least we could turn to people who were directly involved and were helpful by this stage, instead of trying to look after everybody else and not being able to look after our own. (Jack)*

It is now time for professionals to stop ignoring the needs and strengths of fathers. They are also a resource for their children, and possibly for their children's mother too, and they can be powerful advocates. Their position in the eyes of society (as 'Head of the Household') must be challenged when it disempowers mothers and children, but must not be ignored. There must be a more powerful alliance between professionals, survivors, and non-abusing mothers and fathers in order that children might be protected.

# 7

# Conflicts and differences

THERE ARE a variety of differences as well as similarities among non-abusing mothers and fathers, and a range of conflicting agendas to consider when attempting to understand the mothers' and father's experiences. In relation to the different agencies and different workers the parents in this book came into contact with, there were many areas of potential conflict. Different agencies have different policies depending on the type of abuse and 'type' of child. Some agencies regard child sexual abuse as an emergency, responding to it with rigid procedures that they must adhere to. Other agencies regard their response as therapeutic and specialist. All agencies appear to regard extra-familial child sexual abuse differently to intra-familial abuse (Trotter, 1991; Sharland et al, 1995).

Similarly, different professionals regard child sexual abuse differently depending on the agency they work for, and depending on their own personal issues. They may see their involvement as an opportunity for revenge, to punish abusers. Or they may regard their work as an opportunity to save and rescue children. Either position may help them feel better about themselves. Some individuals continue to avoid child sexual abuse, as Mary found,

*'I asked the teachers why they didn't recognise the symptoms, they said they don't like to interfere.* (Mary)

It is also possible that workers may involve themselves in this arena in order to abuse others, '...it was common to take referrals of adolescents who had been abused in local authority foster placements.' (Pringle, 1993, p6).

The Children Act 1989 crystallises a fundamental conflict in child protection as it addresses the dilemma of intervention versus non-intervention. The Act prohibits formal intervention by the making of a court order unless shown to be better for the child than making no order (s.1(5)) and also restricts local authorities' powers to prevent removal of children from its accommodation or control contact to children where a court order has been obtained (ss.20, 34). However, so-called 'voluntary' action may amount to intervention as parents may be overtly or covertly coerced into accepting services to avoid court proceedings or removal of their children.

Agencies may be constrained in their abilities to provide appropriate responses to certain groups of children, or to children who have suffered particular forms of abuse (Burgess et al, 1984; Frenken and Stolk, 1990; Richardson and Bacon, 1991; Westcott, 1993).

Other potentially differing agendas may relate to the child, for example those who are very young or have a disability. Very few professionals are qualified to work with deaf children (Kennedy, 1992), and the different agendas of adults and children generally may lead to conflict (Westcott, 1993) and 'secondary victimisation' (Wells, 1992). Levitt et al (1991) point out that the different service providers often have different agendas for treating victims and their families which may result in intrusive or ill co-ordinated acts and secondary victimisation. They also provide an important reminder that in other cases parents have felt the need to protect their children from abusers when the 'system' has been unable to act.

Three of the mothers (Mary, Alice and Jane) expressed their worries about the safety of other children and felt that little attention was given to this by the professionals.

*I don't know what she's going to be like in a relationship. I'm frightened that she's going to abuse somebody else as well, this is always going through my mind. (Alice)*

*I just feel why should he get away with it? He's just sitting back. He's got a daughter now and he could be interfering with her. It's just totally sick. It's really, really sick. (Mary)*

Taking these, and other considerations into account it is clear to see that services provided by certain specific types of agency or worker might be appropriate for certain specific types of children or for certain specific types of abuse, they might not be appropriate for others. Mothers and fathers have priorities and agendas which differ again. For them child sexual abuse is a series of crises; a lifetime's concern; a shameful, painful, private tragedy (De Jong, 1988).

Staunton and Darling (1992) reported that the mothers they worked with raised a number of issues, including: lack of support by social workers; problems with the legal system; feeling let down and isolated. It is not hard to imagine therefore, given the catalogue of different priorities and agendas, how frequently mothers and fathers might find themselves in a position of conflict with the agencies they become involved with. Such conflicts may be exacerbated if personal conflicts about parenting generally have been unresolved.

## Polarisation and Ambivalence

The pleasure and satisfaction of being a parent has to be balanced against the loss of freedom that parental responsibility brings, 'All parents have to manage some ambivalence towards their children' (Klein, 1959). It can be very difficult to acknowledge anger or negative feelings towards someone who is loved and important, and this is particularly so when that person is a child. The enormity of feelings which may be around following any trauma will be difficult to express and manage; the feelings which may be aroused by the discovery of sexual abuse are possibly even harder to express. Discussion of sexual matters is often forbidden among adults, let alone among children in many families; and issues of loyalty and betrayal may prohibit debate between generations, yet the emotions are experienced by the child(ren) as well as the parents. Feelings can also change and fluctuate.

Melanie Klein has described how babies have to come to terms with their own mixed feelings towards their parents, and to face the depressing fact that the parent who provides the good experience is the same person who is sometimes not there (Klein, 1959). Parents too have to manage mixed feelings. According to Klein, one way that this can happen in families is for feelings to be polarised, so that one person expresses the positive side of feelings and the other is forced to express the negative ones. Where the child has disabilities, their extra dependency can create extreme problems for parents. Similar polarised positions may be experienced by parents who are caring for a child who has been emotionally 'disabled' by sexual abuse.

Things may be further complicated by the fact that the social attributions of different male and female roles and tasks may lead to one partner being more frustrated and less able to deal with it, so the problem may appear to be a marital or health problem (Smith and Breathwick, 1987). Unremitting dependency needs of a sexually abused child may be similar to those of a child with disabilities. If mothers immediately respond (as they are socially conditioned to do) by expressing all the caring, nurturing, 'positive' feelings, are fathers forced into the polarised position of expressing all the 'negative' ones - anger, hatred, revenge, disgust and so on? This did not appear to be the case on the whole for the parents in this book, a more complex mix of positive and negative responses were experienced by all of them.

It may not be parents who deal with their ambivalence about dependency by polarising it; rather it may be the professionals. The study 'Mate and Stalemate' (Mattinson and Sinclair, 1979) gives examples of workers from different agencies identifying with different clients in their conflict. 'Not only is this exhausting and unprofessional, but the clients are not helped to come to terms with their own ambivalence about their needs.' (Smith and Breathwick, 1978, p70).

Susan had an immense amount of ambivalence to deal with. She was confused and distressed by her own severe sexual abuse as a child, and about her husband's sexual and physical abuse of her two sons. This was further compounded by mixed feelings as to the extent of her own responsibility in the abuse. Her husband's family reported worrying behaviour signs in the children, but minimised and dismissed their significance. The professionals she came into contact with showed concern and investigated on more than one occasion, but were unable to confirm that abuse had occurred nor which parent (or grandparent) was responsible. Matthew, Luke and Susan continue to suffer debilitating symptoms related to sexual abuse, and Susan continues to be confused about her feelings.

*I just got totally, totally angry about all this. I just got so sick.*
(Susan)

Hopefully Susan will be able to see some resolution to her confusions and to her and her children's position as she is pursuing legal action against her husband (without the support of child protection agencies).

## Differences between familial and non-familial abuse

One of the major divisions in policies, practice and personal responses relates to whether the abuser was a family member. Professionals may have different policies regarding familial or non-familial abuse. There may be conflict between them regarding this although MacFarlane argued that 'Investigatory procedures and evaluation techniques should be quite similar...' (MacFarlane, 1987, p299).

Services are usually less systematically provided to families where the abuse was non-familial (if at all) after the case conference. Issues of 'need' seem to be less clearly assessed than those of 'protection' by the statutory agencies. Most of the parents in this book expressed a need for more frequent and regular support from professionals following case conference.

The trend to focus on protection of the identified child (and immediate family) is also worrying as many abusers do not confine themselves to one child, or one group of children (Finkelhor, 1986; Driver, 1989; La Fontaine, 1990).

Attempts by researchers to categorise the offenders separately manifestly fail when increasing exposure begins to show that many of them are indiscriminate in their preference for family members or strangers, choosing one or the other simply because of considerations of access or avoidance of detection. (Driver, 1989).

Professionals have tended to try and see familial and non-familial offenders as separate groups - particularly being reluctant to consider that familial offenders may well have abused others outside the family. The mothers and father in this study were aware of these possibilities and in at least two cases tried to alert professionals to their concerns - without success. There were particular difficulties for others regarding the safety of friends or cousins.

*We were concerned that Social Services seemed powerless to act, these other children aren't on the child protection register either. I just hope that we are not right at the expense of one of these other children. (Mary)*

Byerly (1985) in an outline of the needs of mothers whose children have been victims of incest, points out that many mothers feel a desire to protect the abuser, especially if he shows remorse. She suggests that a woman's natural protective and maternal feelings are likely to surface. Mary experienced such feelings but neither she nor Caroline's father, who also felt he should protect the perpetrator, acted on those feelings. Jack, who supposedly does not 'naturally' possess protective and maternal feelings, also felt a desire to protect the abuser, his brother. Most of the mothers however, already disliked the abuser, or were suspicious of him; they had no difficulty with feelings of loyalty.

## Differences between 'purposeful' and accidental disclosures

Enlightenment about a particular episode of sexual abuse may come about in a variety of ways. What has come to be accepted as the most common way for child sexual abuse to be reported is through what Sgroi has termed 'purposeful disclosure' (1982). This is where children make a clear statement about what has happened to them, presumably with an intention of alerting adults and gaining protection. This was the case for five of the children in this study, a similar proportion to that found other studies (Monck, 1989). Five other children however, did not make purposeful disclosures, or rather, none that were heard or believed.

Of the five who seemed to disclose 'purposefully', all of them were, from that time, protected from further abuse by their mothers and fathers, and all but one of them received services which were helpful to them in some ways. It is interesting to note that these five children were abused for a shorter time than the other children.

Whether this was a result of the children's success at disclosure, their parents success at protecting them or the professionals success in intervention cannot be concluded from such a small number.

It is also interesting to observe that four (of the five children who purposefully disclosed), were girls, whereas all five of the accidental disclosures were boys. This may be an indication of a greater willingness to believe girls (on the part of parents, professionals and the children themselves) about sexual abuse, which may or may not be linked to a greater eagerness to protect them. There may also be a connection to the preponderance of

*Availability of fathers*

|  | disclosed to mother | disclosed to father | purposeful disclosure | accidental disclosure |
|---|---|---|---|---|
| Jason | ✓ |  |  | ✓ |
| Dana | ✓ |  | ✓ |  |
| Matthew | ✓ |  |  | ✓ |
| Luke | ✓ |  |  | ✓ |
| Ann | ✓ |  | ✓ |  |
| Caroline | ✓ | ✓ | ✓ |  |
| David | ✓ |  |  | ✓ |
| Ben | ✓ |  | ✓ |  |
| Darren | ✓ |  |  | ✓ |
| Julie | ✓ | ✓ | ✓ |  |
| Totals | 10 | 2 | 5 | 5 |

women in survivors' groups and networks (Bass & Davis, 1989; Danica, 1989).

For the four children who did not make a purposeful disclosure, they were abused for longer, displayed various signs and symptoms of emotional and sexual disturbance, and with only one exception are all still having difficulties and receiving services. In all of these cases the mothers did act to protect their children once the abuse was discovered or identified, and in all but one they were successful. Ending the abuse was on the whole a clear and straightforward task for them. What was much less straightforward was finding appropriate help and advice for their children's and their own recovery.

MacFarlane (1986) advocates a number of responses that parents could adopt when their children disclose to them. These include under-reacting, believing and avoiding blame. Also listed is 'Do not make efforts to bury the incident... or put it behind you... children need to be given the opportunity and the permission to express their feelings as they come up... and to put the abuse in its proper perspective'. (MacFarlane, 1986, p305-306). MacFarlane goes on to point out that trying to silence a child is usually a result of trying to avoid having to hear or think about what they might say. Alice learnt for herself how not to silence Dana.

*By this time I sort of knew how to react to it because of the way I'd* reacted previously (which was completely wrong because she could see the fear on my face. (Alice)

Frequently mothers and fathers were dealing with different agencies and professionals, and receiving little advice. Sometimes they faced conflicting opinions and opposing viewpoints. There does appear to be a correlation between those children in this book who were unable to make purposeful disclosures and the effectiveness of the services they received.

## Separation from abuser

Some of the mothers and the father had difficulties deciding about future contact with the abuser (when he was a family member), particularly in the longer term. For some of them the decision included losing contact with brothers and sisters, mothers and fathers, cousins, Aunts and Uncles as families divided in their beliefs, acceptance and allegiances. The parents did not always find the professionals helpful in this regard.

'Professionals vary in the emphasis they place on separation from the abuser or rehabilitation and mothers often receive mixed and conflicting messages from different individuals and agencies.' (Hooper, 1989, p27). Hooper raises the issue of societal confusion about child sexual abuse, and how this may further confuse mothers in their interaction with agencies. She points to the often conflicting messages between television programmes (advocating togetherness, forgiveness and family reconciliation's) and professionals (who may insist on no further contacts). Other conflicts and confusions also exist (Kitzinger, 1996).

Advice from professionals is even less clear when the abuser is a child in the family. Sally was horrified when advised by the health visitor that the abuse of her youngest son Ben, by his eight year old brother David, had to be reported to the police. The health visitor assured her that the police wouldn't

*...turn up at your door. But they did. I had the police at me door. They wanted to take my two sons away without me, to interview them on a video tape. Well that was it. I couldn't... You know, I was in... I couldn't... I mean...* (Sally)

The mother was also advised that there wouldn't have to be a case conference because the abuse had been between children within the family. She was later told that there had to be a case conference. Sally also had to send Ben to stay with her parents, in order for him to be 'protected' from his brother. Fortunately they were happy to help, Sally was glad of the reduced responsibility and Ben was willing to stay with them.

## Difficult behaviour

All of the mothers and the father in this book reported behaviour that was difficult for them to deal with. For Edith, her son Darren's 'threatened' behaviour was equally difficult and distressing.

*Then he started saying he was going to go on the railway lines to run in front of a train. This is when I was trying to make him do as he was told.* (Edith)

Sally had experienced particularly extreme behaviour problems with her youngest son for two years (despite on-going help from a child psychiatrist).

*...his attitude towards his brother - I mean he stabbed his brother with his knife sitting at the tea table! He destroyed all his brother's board games, he started to wet the bed 2 or 3 times a night, he started to dirty and he spread it up the bedroom door and the wall. One night he got out of bed and went into his brothers' bedroom, dirtied on his brother's quilt while he was asleep in bed, and just calmly went back to bed.* (Sally)

Edith was particularly frustrated by different agencies' refusal to help her because her child used drugs.

*I knew about the sexual abuse then, but I didn't associate it with the drug problem.... I desperately needed help.* (did you get help?) *No. I'm still waiting for it. There is no help for children who have drug problems between the ages of 12 and 16.* (Edith)

Although Edith did get medical help for Darren, (including hospital admissions and a period in a secure unit) she did not feel that the help offered to him was appropriate for a child, and many of the provisions excluded him because of his association with drugs and/or because he smoked.

## Dealing with crises

The mothers and father faced a number of crises as accounts unfolded and events transpired. At times, they were able to find resources within themselves which helped them cope. Sometimes however, they felt unprepared and ill-equipped to deal with crises, as Jack described.

*I had no experience, thankfully, of anything like this at all before. Diana and I were just completely at a loss, our wits were just about shattered.* (Jack)

The range of services offered to the mothers and father were vast, and the majority of the offers were taken up by the families. However many frustrations were expressed and a number of gaps were identified. One of the most common frustrations related to incidents or episodes which were regarded as emergencies by the parents.

A number of researchers (MacLeod and Saraga, 1991; Sharland et al, 1995) suggest that a mother is likely to be in 'shock' on the discovery that her child has been sexually abused, and that it is likely that she will experience the kinds of feelings around in bereavement work. They go no to add that someone in shock is 'highly unlikely to be able to make decisions and assume responsibility' (p40) and workers should not go along with procedures which expect her to do so.

Shock might also be a common reaction for the mothers of abusers, as seemed to be the case for Jack (and Michael's) mother.

*My mother went hysterical, but she went hysterical for..., for not the right reasons as far as I could see. It was all about her. Her first reaction she had was that they were going to take Michael away...* (Jack)

Not all the mothers responded the same way, Mary was particularly calm and organised.

*What I tried to do was to get her just to explain what had happened, and I actually made some notes because I thought something's got to be done about this.* (Mary)

The initial 'emergency' response which centred on investigation

## Conflicts and Differences

by professionals was often much appreciated. Sally found she felt 'wrapped up' in all the immediate urgency of the situation and appreciated all the attention they were getting. Jack reported a very efficient response to their initial referral, which reassured him and Diana. However alter requests for services were not so quickly dealt with.

*Nothing happened for about six or seven weeks. Then we went back to our GP and said look, we were really worried.* (Jack)

For Jane and Mary there seemed to be a second crisis point for them and their children. Jane said this was following the investigative interview by a police officer and a social worker. Jane felt that she was unprepared for such a flow of emotion and distress from Jason all over again and the officers' announcement, as they were leaving, that a hospital appointment had been made for an examination the following day proved to be a further catalyst.

Mary reported a second crisis following a chance remark by a younger daughter which triggered renewed feelings of guilt for Caroline.

*Once we were all sitting watching this family video, and the little one had said when am I going back to my Aunties? She (Caroline) had just gone off and broken her heart... She must have sneaked back down, and she consumed about half a bottle of Bacardi. That was the night I found her with her arms cut, collapsed in the bathroom, sobbing her heart out for her nanna. So I just whipped her straight up to the casualty department.* (Mary)

What professionals defined as an emergency did not always coincide with what the parents felt were crises. Edith attempted to get urgent help for Darren who was violent and suicidal, during a weekend.

*The first doctor I called out... was a locum. He took three hours to come out and when he actually got there he said he wasn't qualified to deal with it, take him to the surgery on Monday! Which was no help at all. The second doctor that I called out he took an hour and a half to come, but he quite obviously was experienced. He tried to have him admitted to..., he phoned... they said he really needed to be in touch with the child psychiatrist, but he couldn't get him. Eventually the casualty officer said he would see, but to be quite honest he was quite calm by the time they got to see him. I mean they didn't see him like he was.* (Edith)

## Services provided and services needed

On many occasions mothers and father referred to 'waiting' for services.

*He's been referred to the ...unit, he psychiatrist there said it was a hard decision but they would have him for an assessment. But it would only be a four week assessment, and not until the next year, because there's a waiting list. And of course, Darren doesn't really want to go there now because, again, its a no-smoking unit.* (Edith)

*I went to see his teacher who recommended an Educational Psychologist be called in. Between you and me we're still waiting!* (Jane)

These periods of 'waiting' were even at the initial referral stage for Jane and Alice, times which they found immensely distressing for themselves and their children.

*At 8.30am I phoned the doctor's and I told her what had happened. She said Oh crumbs, hang on, someone will be with you in 24-48 hours, we'll get back to you. So then I rung the headmaster at his school and told him what had happened. He said it was very good I'd informed but he had no option but to follow procedures and inform social services and police. He apologised for having to do it but I said no, do it, do it! Again he assured me that someone would be out in 24-48 hours to see me and Jason to get the story. This 24-48 hours actually turned out to be seven days!* (Jane)

When the police did eventually arrive, Jason would no longer speak about the abuse. His 'moment of crisis' had been a week before.

Alice and Jack felt that the system was poorly co-ordinated and not designed to meet needs.

*We were messed about for two weeks, appointments changed and so on - it was very awkward with school and my work. I had to change appointments and lie to my customers... We waited six months for an appointment with a child psychiatrist.* (Alice)

*...she's not equipped to give you in a ten minute appointment... so she wrote to Social Services. The letter was pushed around from desk to desk. Christmas was looming and Diana and I were very unhappy about the way things were going... The story about different departments, I had wrote to the head of the case conference, and he had dished it to somebody else.* (Jack)

Jane felt that an almost 'automatic' application of investigative procedures ignored the timing of the disclosure in relation to the abuse, and caused additional and unnecessary distress.

*We went down to the doctor... I was so frightened and Jason was absolutely terrified. I tried to assure him the doctor just wants to check you're OK. But I had to say something, they were just abusing him again. I said look it's two years since this happened, you're just abusing him again. She said 'I agree with you but the social workers need it for their records.* (Jane)

Some mothers did appreciate the help that professionals offered, but thought that this was rarely at the times when they most needed it, as Mary clearly describes.

*He (the social worker) actually rang me, says how you doing?, I said OK, but I thought, you can be alright when you get a phone call when you're at work and trying to function, you can think you're alright, but is when you're feeling real crap in the middle of the night, that's the hard bit.* (Mary)

Staunton and Darling's report (1992) revealed further issues about timing. The mothers in their groups felt that the leaders' flexibility with regard to timings of the sessions was very helpful, and 'weekly, for one and half hours' was felt to be about right. However the break (of one month in the summer) was not regarded as helpful, and one of the two groups wanted the sessions to continue 'indefinitely' (instead of ending after 18 months).

These mothers also felt a strong need for individual and group sessions, and that one should not be a substitute for the other. Staunton and Darling emphasise the enormous amount of time needed in order to do this work. It was not common for the mothers and father in this book to complain that the professionals were not trained to help them, as Driver and

Droisen suggested. 'When we got to the doctor's he said he didn't know what to do and he had never heard of anything like it. He wanted to know if it was wise for him to examine the children... He examined them and said, 'I don't think anything is broken, do you?' (Mrs Sullivan in Driver & Droisen, 1989, p79). However, Jane complained that the social worker did not have enough time to help her or Jason.

*A social worker eventually appeared from nowhere on the Monday and started saying we all believe you and it's not your fault etc. I thought what a load of shit! But then I thought give him a break. I said he's been crying and crying, you've no idea what that kid's been through, no one deserves it. He didn't want to hear, he backed off. He said he needed to go, he had an appointment and away he went.* (Jane)

The mothers in Staunton and Darling's study all thought that a service based in their own community was not helpful, they preferred the anonymity the hospital provided (Staunton and Darling, 1992). In contrast Alice complained of a lack of local services, and lack of facilities for children.

*...miles away, no arrangement to look after Dana while I talked (although I'd said on the phone I wanted to talk privately), no equipment for Dana to play with, Dana didn't like him (or the lack of toys).* (Alice)

Alice was also frustrated by her own unhappy experiences with the agencies.

*I went to a GP for advice and help. He told me all his personal problems. I went to a victim support group but it wasn't regular or very good for me.* (Alice)

Frustrations which were shared by professionals were also expressed, for example the slowness of legal procedures.

*'It's taken four and a half years to get my case to court, even if it takes us another four and a half years to fight for my sons, I'll do it.* (Susan)

The most flexible and readily available source of support in times of crisis was provided by informal networks. Most of the mothers had friends or relatives to turn to, and on the whole they seemed to be available when they were needed.

*I rang my friend up and she came down like a shot.* (Jane)

## Communication and information

On occasions misunderstandings and misinterpretations caused conflicts between mothers and professionals. Edith found it particularly difficult to agree with various professionals about Darren's needs and about her own abilities to provide care for him.

*So they adjourned for seven days. I said ...and what are you going to do with him for seven days? They said you can take him home. I said I'm not taking him home in that state. I said I didn't get him like that. In that case, they said, put him in care. I said I'm not going to give him to you because he'll just run away. I said you let them run away. He said we don't let them, but I said you can't stop them. He says in that case I'm going back into court now for an emergency protection order. I said well you do that because I'm not going to give my son to you.* (Edith)

This apparently deadlocked dialogue illustrates the frustrations and difficulties that can arise between individuals and organisations. Neither 'side' were prepared to concede failure in their attempts to help Jason in the past. Edith continued to stick up for herself and Darren in the face of daunting adversaries.

Hooper (1989) suggests that the complex and often conflictual messages mothers are giving about themselves, should be heard for their own sake, not only as appropriate or inappropriate reactions to the child. She goes on the say that the coping strategies women adopt in response to the threat to themselves may be a source of some of the behaviour professionals describe as 'lack of co-operation' with the intervention process. Hooper goes on to add that recognising these behaviours as coping strategies might not make things easier for the professionals or for the child, but they do not equate with condoning the abuse or not caring for the child.

Edith's position in her discussion with professionals may have been more about overcoming feelings of powerlessness than about actual institutions or particular legalities; and certainly were not about negating her responsibilities or care for Darren.

Mary persuaded professionals to understand and accept what she thought were her daughter's needs, by securing the support of another professional.

> ...the school were saying you're going to have to get her back into school. I'm saying, not until she's ready, if she can't cope, I won't force the issue. So actually I went to see my GP and we got a letter from her to say that she was under a lot of pressure and she could do without any more. (Mary)

Offering evaluations and conflicting opinions among professionals can result in flawed decisions being made (Kelly & Milner, 1996), and may also influence the amount of information made available to parents. Levitt and her colleagues (1991) found that primary care-givers (mothers, fathers and other relatives) of sexually abused children valued highly agencies which provided needed information and workers who explained things. This was an issue for Susan and Mary, poor practice was reported when their workers did not provide enough information.

> I went to see a social worker and told her what had happened. She came out and talked to my husband and they took him (Matthew) for an examination, but they wouldn't tell us what had happened... When we went to the clinic he (Matthew) was gone for ages, they gave him a damn good examination. Whey wouldn't they tell us anything about it? I asked my son what they had done, and he said they had looked at his back end. (Susan)

> ...it seemed to drag on for weeks and whilst they said we'll keep you informed, nothing seemed to be happening and I kept having to ring them up and ask. (Mary)

Byerly (1985) acknowledges such difficulties for mothers and accepted that they worry about their children's reactions and subsequent feelings and behaviour. She advises her readers to consult recommended books, to talk to rape crisis counsellors, or to talk to other experienced mothers. Most of the mothers and the father in this book took numerous opportunities to find out what they could about child sexual abuse generally and about child abuse in their own families, although Alice felt that she shouldn't have to.

## Conflicts and Differences

*It seemed as though everything I had to find out myself.* (Alice)

Hooper (1989) points out that there are sources of information both inside and outside a family. Sources of information from within the family include signs and behaviours of family members as well as spoken information such as disclosures or confessions. Sources of information from outside a family are often general information about sexual abuse from the media or from friends or family. Hooper found that mothers who already had some suspicion or knowledge could find that public information was helpful to her for reinterpreting events and taking action.

Hooper did not find that public information about child sexual abuse was particularly helpful to those mothers who did not already suspect something, and things which professionals might recognise as clear indicators might not be recognised as such by mothers, except with hindsight. This point seemed to apply to Mary and Jack.

*I was absolutely appalled because I recognised so much of what was on that page: mood swings, temper tantrums, truancy, behavioural exploits, later on she did ...razor blade..., drinking - alcohol abuse, personality change, she wasn't sleeping. I mean I hadn't realised how bad it was. At one time I used to tell her off for saying she was going to bed at 10 o'clock, then I'd go up at half past 11 or midnight and she was still dressed. I hadn't realised obviously she was frightened of going to bed, nightmares and all of this stuff.* (Mary)

*So obviously we talked to Julie, we tried to reassure her, everything's going to be alright, but we were talking about seeing Michael and talking things out... We said that with the best of intentions, obviously we later gathered that it wasn't the thing to do.* (Jack)

Practical information about what to do or about resources available were valued highly by the mothers and father in this book, but much of this was gathered much later or just by chance.

*I had thought that Rape Crisis was only rape victims, it was just a chance remark that I heard that. So I wrote to them.* (Mary)

The mothers in Staunton and Darling's paper (1992) felt that the lack of information was a major issue for them. Information about each individual case and how it was progressing, and what decisions had been made were also of crucial importance to the mothers in this book. The control of information was also an issue for Mary.

> *Initially we didn't want any of the other teachers to know, but that in itself was causing problems. She (Caroline) was going to school and having problems, and she was getting hassled to do her homework. Well if she didn't feel like doing it, I wasn't forcing her to do it. So after a long discussion with the Education Welfare Officer and her Head of Year, we decided that we would actually let her teachers know what the problem had been. I think a lot of them assumed she'd probably been off pregnant and had an abortion, which is the usual reason for unexplained absences.* (Mary)

Byerly (1985) found that most mothers needed information regarding their rights; information on sexual and other forms of abuse (including domestic violence); information and advice about procedures and options in the system generally; medical and psychological information, and tips about survival and stress management. They commonly asked about effects and treatments for their children (abused children and siblings), and whether their child enjoyed the sex (Byerly, 1985, p29). They also needed to know how and when to talk about the abuse, and who with; how to regain trust and openness in the family; how to protect their children in the future and whether life will ever return to normal.

Alice was particularly glad she had access to legal advice and information as, without it, she felt that Dana's name would have been placed on the register. Most of the mothers and father in this book wished they had known more in order to better help their children, if not to have protected them from the abuse ever happening.

> *I feel very strongly that there should be some campaigns to make parents more aware, you know, because until that time... I could have done such a lot more.* (Mary)

## Family conflict

All of the mothers and the father experienced conflicts within their own families. Jack felt divided in his loyalties between his brother and mother, and his daughter.

## Conflicts and Differences

*I was torn between trying to protect me brother, because it was me brother. But what became apparent, it wasn't sinking in to my mother. She didn't seem to be accepting things in one sense, but even though she was going hysterical. After about an hour I said mother, you never once asked how Julie is! It became as plain as... you know, she didn't ask how Julie was.* (Jack)

It was not uncommon for different members of families to view things differently. Susan and Alice experienced extreme conflict, and Susan proved her feelings by attacking her husband.

*...I got really violent, really, really violent towards my husband. I used to really do some horrible things; I used to physically attack him. He used to curl up in a little ball he was so frightened of us, my temper.* (Susan)

Mary was able to control her inclination for conflict for the sake of her family.

*He said 'if your mother was sitting there, and he (the abuser) was tied to a chair and they gave her a revolver, she'd shoot him as well; and you would.' I said 'I wouldn't, I'd like to, but I wouldn't' because, again, where would the family be without me, where would I be without them.* (Mary)

Edith experienced conflict with Darren, and found it difficult to use her authority, especially when she felt this was undermined by the professionals.

*That is currently the problem I still have with him. He's nearly 15, and if I say to him, right bed, he'll say I'm not going to bed. I'll say, oh but you are. Or he'll say I'm not going to school today, and I'll say oh but you are. He'll say you can't make us, and I'll say oh but I can. ...in situations like ours where Darren has his own children's social worker and I have an adult social worker, because he was told he was his own person and nobody could tell him what he had to do, his life was his to do what he wanted with it. But somewhere along the line somebody forgot to tell him he still had a mother, and he still had a dad who have rights and are able to tell him he's got to do things.* (Edith)

Managing and resolving these conflicts was often difficult. Alice, who disagreed with her mother's advice about talking to

Dana, found day-to-day business difficult.

*I talk to her a lot about things, my Mum says I shouldn't ...all through this I've had to go out to work. Its been really hard, to be happy and talk to your customers about what they want to hear. You're feeling absolutely miserable inside.* (Alice)

Mary adopted a number of strategies to help herself and her family cope with conflict.

*obviously he (Caroline's father) was very traumatised by that at the time, but when he calmed down he actually appreciated that if we hadn't taken the time to sort of build a protective barrier round him and be there for him, (he stayed with us for a few days), he reckons he probably would have gone and killed him (the abuser).*
*(who did you lean on?) Well I didn't have anyone to lean on at the time. Once, when it got a bit much, I slammed the front door, got into the car and went away and drove and cried at the sea on a rainy day. Blew everything away.* (Mary)

## Bridges and alliances

As mentioned earlier, Levitt and her colleagues (1991) found that the depletion of income and resources (as a result of both marital breakdown and the expenses of services and treatments), was of great significance to parents. Other concerns reported by these parents were that services were often fragmented and inconsistent, and usually too short-term. Levitt et al found that what was helpful to families was a comprehensive medical evaluation, appropriate referral on (to counselling, social or legal services), and on-going support for one care-giver. Their survey revealed that the services that received the highest ratings were the evaluating physician, victim and witness assistance services, guardians ad litem, and professional counselling services. (Levitt and her colleagues do go on to point out that counselling was often found to be less than helpful a) as some parents were restricted by their prepaid health insurance programmes in their choice of counsellor and b) some counsellors lacked expertise in this area).

For the parents in this book, the availability of support (professional or otherwise) was crucial. Similarly, Byerly put 'someone to talk to' at the top of the list and 'someone to counsel me about my own incest' second in importance, for the mothers in her book. (Byerly, 1985, p15).

More than one of the mothers in this book expressed a need to channel their emotions and use their knowledge and experiences in some positive direction.

*What I feel now is that I've got all this anger in me, this energy, instead of spending it being angry at something I can't do anything about I'd rather channel it into something I can do something about. By joining this group at least I can join the ranks of those who want to do something for a change. I've just started a Counselling Skills course, so that eventually if parents want to come and talk I'll be willing to talk to them. I'm a bit anxious about whether I could cope with their needs, so I thought the course would be helpful.* (Mary)

Staunton and Darling point out that as clients are likely to perceive things differently (despite having many issues in common with others), it is essential for workers to consult them on their views of the service they have received; 'what we as therapists think is good for clients, is not necessarily the case.' (Staunton and Darling, 1992). Consulting and involving survivors is beginning to be recognised as a valuable part of providing effective services (Taylor-Browne, 1997; Valente & Borthwick, 1995) and is likely to be one of the most influential developments for future practice.

# 8
# Implications for practice

THIS CHAPTER attempts to draw together some of the main conclusions that the mothers and father came to themselves, and presents them, with some of my own, as a starting place for further research, discussion and development. I hope that the individual testimonies of the parents in previous chapters have been helpful to practitioners who need to increase their range of understanding and awareness of mothers and fathers. I also hope that it has been of interest to other non-abusing mothers and fathers by sharing and comparing experiences. While it is not my intention to draw categorical general conclusions in this chapter, I hope that practitioners will be informed and alerted to possible ways of improving their work with their clients.

## Treatment in Partnership

As most of the mothers and the father in this study were able (sometimes with the help and support of family and friends) to protect their own children, they looked to the many services that were offered to them for help with the aftermath of the abuse. Some of them specifically looked for 'treatment' for their children and themselves. What should they have expected?

Treatment efforts in general, have been found to be of varying success (Cohn & Daro, 1987; Gough, 1993). Cohn and Daro's study of the relative effectiveness of different approaches to treatment (eighty-nine programmes in the USA) suggests however, greater success with problems of sexual abuse than with other forms of abuse or neglect. The treatments were notably lay counselling and group services, including Parents Anonymous, group therapy and parent education classes. I suggest that the successes were due to the involvement of parents and lay people (and possibly to the less prominent involvement of

## Implications for Practice

professionals), and these might have been even greater if mothers and fathers (and particularly fathers) had been separately addressed in the research as well as in the individual programmes.

The 'treatment' that the mothers and father in this study received for themselves and for their children varied enormously and was regarded by them with an almost equal variety of enthusiasm. There did not appear to be any consistency between the 'treatments' offered, although individual work with the children featured to some extent, for all the families.

In California, a comprehensive treatment response (to intrafamilial sexual abuse) has been developed by Giarretto (1982). Gillies (1991) outlines the three parts to the model; the professional component, the community support\controls, and the self help component (also known as 'parents united'). The model was designed (and is used) with a basic premise that on the whole, children do better with their families. One of their main aims is to allow the victim to remain at home.

Whether their supposition about what's 'best' for children is correct or not, their focus on the child's home increases the involvement and importance of those at and near home or family. The self-help component is an essential part of the programme, and includes mutual support and 'sponsorship', support for mothers, offenders and children, educational activities, social and fund-raising activities and a crisis response service. Gillies emphasises the non-judgemental acceptance of offenders in the programme as 'they are not seen as sexual molesters but as parents who have molested their children'. (Gillies, 1991, p173).

This controversial approach heralds a shift in focus which may be uncomfortable to many people who are aware of other issues, not least of all to survivors. Research suggests that many abusers do not confine themselves to children within one family (Lanning and Burgess, 1984; Finkelhor, 1986), nor to one episode of abuse (Finkelhor, 1986) nor are they reluctant to 'share' their victims with other abusers (La Fontaine, 1990; Tate, 1991). The California model does however, force us to remember that fathers (step-fathers) continue to be fathers (step-fathers) even when they have abused; and that there may be non-abusing mothers (step-mothers), fathers (step-fathers), grandmothers (step-grandmothers), grandfathers (step-grandfathers), sisters (step-sisters) and brothers (step-brothers) to work alongside. All of these relatives, and others, would be considered for inclusion in the programmes to help with protection and recovery for the 'victim' and the family.

In the United Kingdom the emphasis on 'working together' with parents (DHSS & Welsh Office, 1988) has confirmed a crucial component of 'good practice', or what the parents might see as 'treatment'. The Department of Health stresses (Department of Health, 1989b) that usually the most effective way of providing help for children, is to develop a good working partnership with the child's parents (1989a, page 8 principle 7). The concept of 'partnership' features in the White Paper that preceded the Children Act 1989, and in the Department of Health's introductory guide, its guidance and accompanying regulations, and its publications about child-care principles and practice, although the word is not actually used in the Act, nor does it appear to extend to family members other than parents on the whole.

Rowe (1991) is quoted as saying 'We can do much to improve services to children by changing our attitudes to their parents. Parents can be partners....The family's potential as a resource has only just begun to be realised'. (Tunnard, 1991, p4). Tunnard goes further and adds that workers should also draw on the collective experience of members of the community as an additional resource and potential 'partner'. Although a number of the mothers and the father in this book had found themselves networks and self-help groups to turn to in their communities, these had not been suggested to them by the workers they came into contact with.

Cooper (1993) writes 'Partnership between the state and parents is now on the official child-care agenda' (p5), and wonders whether it is a pragmatic proposition or a political statement. Cooper's own motivation (political or otherwise) for exploring issues relating to parents is not clear. His research in this area seems to rely heavily on the work of PAIN (Parents Against INjustice), and his proposition that extreme hostility towards abusers (expressed by some professionals) may have been inspired by feminists, is misguided. His conclusions about parents in partnership with professionals are gloomy.

*The events of the last twenty years have greatly undermined the image of child protection workers as offering a service to and in agreement with families. Instead they are likely to be seen as official intruders, remote and suspicious. (Cooper, 1993, p78).*

None of the parents in this book described their relationships with the workers they came into contact with as 'partnerships', and their descriptions of the relationships did not resemble partnerships. However Cooper's conjecture as to how families might regard child protection workers was not born out here. The mothers and father in this book, with perhaps only one exception, found workers to be hard-working and professional. 'Suspicion' (presumably about whether or not parents had sexually abused their children themselves), was a feature for Susan, but this was not the experience of the others.

The parents in this book could not have aligned themselves with PAIN as they did not regard workers as 'intruding'. Without exception they wanted more rather than less intervention. As far as they could see their children's rights were not in conflict with their own and they should have felt able to embrace the 'partnership' principle of the Children Act, and work with professionals. Unfortunately the reality was not quite like this.

The mothers and father in this book were not concerned with the Children Act, and it was only mentioned by Edith in relation to how it had prevented workers providing a service for Darren against his wishes.

*Then he decided he didn't want to go ... because of the new Children Act, they couldn't make him. (Edith)*

Similarly, as mentioned earlier, the notion of 'partnership' did not present itself. Presumably the great importance that this concept has for professionals was not shared with parents who were not aware of any publications or information guides produced by the Department of Health for their benefit. Perhaps it is not surprising to learn that professionals are finding difficulties with 'partnership'; parents don't know about it.

## Planning for Diversity and Change

The mothers and father in this book found that different workers adopted different styles in their treatment and approach. They met a variety of individuals, some of whom they felt to be extremely helpful and caring, others were less so. On the whole though, they were grateful for the services they received and, as stated earlier, wanted more rather than less intervention.

Whilst the mothers and father were not surprised to find they had a wide variety of individuals and services to deal with, the professionals themselves seemed less adaptable. Understanding the variety of situations that mothers and fathers of sexually abused children find themselves in, is something which professionals have failed to do for some time. Understanding, which in this sense includes compassion and an element of erudition, is clearly crucial for professionals who wish to supply good practice, yet for many reasons, they have continued to stereotype, patronise, disregard and dismiss parents.

In a study undertaken in 1984, Myer and her colleagues found that mothers (of daughters who had experienced sexual abuse by their fathers or father surrogates) '...could not be treated as a homogeneous group'. (Myer, 1984, p49). They differed in many respects: personality characteristics, their initial responses to the revelation of incest, their ability to protect their children, their ability to maintain the family unit, their ability to use treatment, and in their attitudes to children, partners and their own mothers.

Myer makes a number of important points about implications for practice arising from her study. Firstly, because the mothers do not form a homogeneous group, workers must be careful in their assessments and planning for intervention. Secondly, stereotyped ideas must be avoided and mothers' initial response (to the revelation of incest) may change outcomes must not be predicted and plans should not be made based on initial reactions.

*'When a mother is told ...... the first reactions are often shock and denial. Clinicians have no difficulty accepting such a response as a defense when it occurs in relation to loss or death, but may find it hard to accept when sexual abuse is the event. Yet the defense serves the same purpose in both cases. (Myer, 1984, p55)*

As well as understanding the differences between individual mothers and individual fathers, and between different situations and over time, workers must also understand their own individual motives and situations. According to Frenken and Stolk (1990), workers can get caught between their personal inability to go more deeply into the matter and strong professional\policy inclinations to deal with the here and now. Decisions (or contracts) to proceed along the lines of obvious behaviour difficulties, currently experienced emotions, financial or legal worries, or practical matters, are readily made. Focusing on deeper, emotional and often painful issues (for worker as well as client), is less easily accepted. The examples given earlier illustrate the tendency for some professionals to leave the difficult and painful issues to be 'sorted out' by the families in this book.

Frenken and Stolk (1990) suggest that these decisions are based on defensive motives from both workers and (in their case) survivors, and actually hindered information being shared and prevented disclosures. 'They were united in silence regarding the incest'. (p262). Some of the mothers and the father in this book felt they were 'left' to get on with this side of the work and again, wanted more rather than less intervention. However, none of them reported feeling that they or their children were discouraged from speaking about what had happened.

It is crucial for workers to realise that not only do mothers and fathers request this type of work, they ought to be provided with it. 'The support each child received from a close adult following the disclosure of the molestation affected the degree of conflict faced by each child which, in turn, effected the defense mechanisms employed'. (Adams-Tucker, 1986, p77).

However, it is not enough for a mother or father to believe and protect their child, this alone does not necessarily prevent the development of psychological problems for the child. '...a mother's expression of concern about the child and ability to take action to protect her child did not necessarily shield the child from the harmful psychological consequences of the sexual abuse. Positive responses on the part of the mother were not systematically related to the amount of distress the child experienced' (Gomes-Schwartz et al, 1990, p99). Given that mothers and fathers can face a whole range of emotional and practical difficulties when they learn about the sexual abuse of their child, it is likely that they may prioritise some of these over others, to avoid being overwhelmed by problems.

Berliner (1991a) points out that workers may be so focused on the abuse that they may neglect all the difficulties the parent(s) are struggling with. She suggests this is an anomaly for workers in the area of child sexual abuse. 'It is salutary to remember that in other areas ... usually the focus is not on what happened, but on determining what is the problem for the child and family and how help might best be offered' (Berliner, 1991a, p31).

Problem-centred and client-centred approaches are certainly not new (Perlman, 1957; Rogers, 1951) and have proven successful from clients' perspectives (Mayer and Timms, 1970) and Blume's model (1990) for working with adult survivors of incest focuses on the survivor's definitions of problems or 'consequences' and might therefore be regarded as 'inner child-centred'. Problem-centred approaches which are also child-centred however, are less common, although there have been some attempts to address this (Crompton, 1990; Butler & Williamson, 1994). Perhaps the testimonies of the mothers and father in this book suggest that an approach which allows for more than one problem to be centred on, might be more helpful.

Elsewhere Berliner (1991b) suggests that in order to help families support their sexually abused child, workers should adopt a response which allows a direct and explicit exposure of the child's experience and minimises the tendency to avoid or deny that experience. 'This may be accomplished by having the child describe the experience to his or her parents either in person or in written or videotaped communication.' (Berliner, 1991b, p36). Combining this 'confrontational' approach in a child-centred way may pose difficulties if the child does not wish others to know, or does not see that this will address their problems. However, were videotaping or writing to parents a less unusual occurrence for children generally (for example if it were part of school curriculum or youth club activities), abused children might more easily accept it.

Parton (1989) advocates that 'To have the best chance of preventing....child abuse...is to improve and develop universal, non-stigmatizing services which are integrated into the mainstream of social provision for all children'. (p69) Improving communication between children and adults generally might be a worthwhile provision, with the focus on adults, especially those adults who are parents\carers and particularly those parents\carers who are men.

Another factor which workers may often misunderstand is that things are likely to change over time. Bowlby (1969) observed that attachment behaviour of adults and children grows stronger during times of trouble or crisis. This certainly appeared to be born out by the mothers and father in this study. Yet many workers are likely to be familiar with research which suggests that at the time of disclosure or discovery of sexual abuse, when all the family needs to increase attachments, some mothers respond with disbelief or blame (Herman, 1981; Summit, 1983). As mentioned earlier, professionals need to make regular (or on-going) and careful assessments of the relationships between children and parents to account for changes over time.

Faller (1990) purports that, among intrafamilial cases of abuse, maternal support of the child was found to vary according to the mother's relationship with the perpetrator, mothers being most supportive when they are separated or divorced from the perpetrator. Similarly, Berliner (1991) suggests that the closer the relationship with the abuser, the greater the probability that maternal support will be compromised. Although there are a number of problems associated with over-simplistic views about 'choices', issues of attachment and allegiance are relevant. Berliner also found that divided loyalty was a particularly difficult issue for parents when the victim and abuser were siblings. 'Conscientious parents who wish to support a victimised child as well as the abusive child may try to diminish the seriousness of the impact on the victim as well as the seriousness of the abuser's behaviour.....one child is chosen to receive the bulk of support and the other child is expelled from the family.' (Berliner, 1991, p38).

Others (Kikuchi, 1995; Hawkes et al, 1997) have identified divisions among professionals in this area, many expressing reluctance or ambivalence about working with child perpetrators. Sally certainly struggled with these dilemmas in relation to Ben and David, but received little acknowledgement or help with the problem from professionals. Whilst divided loyalties was a difficulty for some of the other mothers and the father in this study, on the whole it did not appear to compromise the safety of the children, nor the level of support they received from their non-abusing parent(s). However, yet again, some of them wanted more rather than less help and advice around this issue.

*Parents also need a lot more help in, we used to tell them, how to control their children. With mine there was violence, I mean there was a lot of violence in him. How was I supposed to control these violent attacks? How was I supposed to divert it into something else? I don't know. I still don't know. I just have to go on with the situation the way it is and hope I'm doing the best thing. (Edith)*

According to Berliner (1991) most parents do believe and support their children and are receptive to educational efforts to improve their response. The special, individual qualities of each non-abusing mother and father should be acknowledged, valued, maximised and used in the work with children who have been sexually abused. 'Recognition of individual maternal response is essential to providing appropriate supportive care for the child victim and the mother while making optimal use of limited resources. (De Jong, 1988, p20). Similarly, the special, individual qualities of each father should be acknowledged, valued, maximised and used in the work with children who have been sexually abused.

## Research and Training

As already pointed out in chapter three, researchers have spent very little time studying mothers or fathers, and virtually none at all regarding non-abusing mothers and fathers. The Department of Health funded a study of the perspectives of parents suspected of abuse (Cleaver & Freeman, 1995) which provided details of 30 families (61 children) in relation to race and social class, but not gender. Professional training, particularly since the Children Act, has done a little more, but on the whole, continues to address 'parents' as a united couple or to consider mostly mothers. On the whole, professional training fails to integrate the different perspectives that are crucial to understanding and intervening in child sexual abuse work (Hirst & Cox, 1996).

Recently, because of the influence of the Children Act and the Department of Health's Guidance, professional training has focused on 'partnership' as the way to work with parents. According to a training pack produced for professionals by the Open University, partnership means 'listening to parents and taking their concerns and priorities seriously'. (Rogers, Roche and Dickerson, 1991, p16).

The pack advises workers to recognise that while not all parents have the skill or patience to care for their child, many may still care about their child. The training does not appear to acknowledge that one parent may have different skills or levels of patience than another. Nor does it recognise that the abilities and attitudes of either parent may change and develop over time; this is despite the obvious acceptance that it takes professionals time (and lengthy training packs) to develop sufficient skills to work with the same children.

Another training pack produced by the National Children's Bureau (Adcock, White and Hollows, 1991), emphasises the importance of a 'shared understanding of what is meant by partnership' (p2) and goes on to look at the development of such notions as involvement, joint planning and conflict management. While this training pack does acknowledge the need for a shift in attitudes as well as in procedures and actions, it does not suggest how parents might get into a position of 'shared understanding either with the professionals, or with each other. Indeed the pack fails to recognise that parents' wishes and views may differ from each other.

One training pack does specifically focus on fathers. A chapter by Peter Marsh in the Family Rights Group training pack acknowledges that fathers have been neglected by social workers in the past and suggests that services should be publicised and information provided to them (Marsh, 1991). Unfortunately he does not distinguish between abusing and non-abusing fathers, nor does he make any suggestion as to how social workers should begin to engage them.

Cooper (1993) refers to a case study in the Open University training pack which he used with final year social work students. Almost all of them failed to consider the father in the case, except for those who assumed him to be the abuser. Whilst Jack (the only father in this book) did not report any feelings of being suspected or accused of being the abuser of his daughter, I feel that it is likely to remain a common assumption among workers that fathers are guilty.

I have suggested that non-abusing parents might benefit themselves from some training in order to help them manage their own feelings and to help them care for their children. The Department of Health advocates specialist preparation and training for foster parents who are caring for sexually abused children (Department of Health, 1991), it seems illogical that birth parents should not need such training, especially as they might have less knowledge and experience of child abuse generally, and also they do not have the luxury of time for preparation.

Foster parent training (for carers of sexually abused children) could be adapted. This might be offered to carers\parents together, and to women\mothers and men\fathers separately. Parents themselves might do the training (with or without professionals). Without exception, the parents in this book wanted more help rather than less, and three of them (Jane, Mary and Sally) are now offering help to others (counselling, training and supporting professionals and non-professionals).

As a further support to the improvement of practice, research also needs to be redirected and extended. Research which includes non-abusing mothers and fathers (and particularly more fathers), needs to be undertaken. Empirical evidence regarding the outcome and effectiveness of interventions, (whether for protection, treatment or prevention) is urgently needed, and to be fully effective this needs to include non-abusing parents (and possibly children too) in the planning, design, undertaking and evaluation stages. Such research might have resulted in a greater use of groups, or a more flexible response to crises; both developments would have been helpful to the mothers and father in this book.

Standardised instruments to measure variables at the beginning and end of protective strategies or treatments, and before and after prevention programmes, should be used. Such research may have meant that Alice and some of the others were not left with as many problems unaddressed. Control or comparison groups should be used wherever possible, this practice might minimise stereotyping and discriminatory practice. Professionals and practitioners should also be involved in the design, implementation and analysis of research; and dissemination of findings and recommendations should be made accessible to as wide an audience as possible (including children themselves). Research findings which are disseminated into convenient formats (booklets, leaflets, posters, videos etc) for statutory and voluntary organisations to pass on, would have been immensely helpful to Alice and Sally. Jane has spent much of her spare time lately, developing and publishing such leaflets.

One commendable piece of research about non-abusing mothers has been published and the experiences of the mothers in this book corroborate many of its findings. Hooper (1992) found, for example, that the availability of support, information and advice were important to mothers, and not always supplied by agencies and workers. Hooper also emphasised the difficulties caused by policy documents, including the Children Act 1989, failing to distinguish between abusing and non-abusing parents. Hooper also advocates training and education for mothers, and for other non-professionals who share in the protection of children.

Stevenson (1991) felt that, '... prompted ... by the concern about sexual abuse, social workers have rushed to 'observe' children's play with little open discussion of the justification for the inferences drawn'. I feel that workers have also 'rushed' into partnership with parents without reflection on the lack of research on non-abusing parents and what this might mean. A more open discussion of research findings about non-abusing mothers and non-abusing fathers is needed before training programmes are designed and good practice established.

*Implications for Practice*

# Power and Powerlessness

Issues of power and powerlessness have emerged throughout this book, and are of central concern to those who are interested in improving practice in the future. Power is not a fixed or static concept, and is perceived and used (and misused) differently by different people. At various points in time a number of the parents in this book perceived the statutory agencies as having a lot of power, as Susan regularly felt, yet at other times they seemed weak.

*We were concerned that Social Services seemed powerless to act ....*
*(Jack).*

On occasions the power of Local Authorities is restricted (for example by s.1(5) of the Children Act which prevents removal of children from its accommodation or controls contact to children), but attempts by legislators to redress some of these power imbalances (by increasing parental 'rights, powers, responsibilities and duties') have not been wholly successful. Milner (1992) confirmed that the child protection procedures pull mothers into the system and push fathers into the background, and others (Hooper, 1992; Trotter, 1997) have added that their rights and powers are subsequently lost or diluted, as well as their responsibilities and duties to their children.

The Central Council for Education and Training in Social Work (1991) advocates 'empowerment' as a key element for redressing power imbalances in practice. White (1990) suggests that empowerment means different things to different people, and this is largely dependent on which people are to be empowered. White separately addresses four groups of people in his discussion: parents, staff, children and politicians. He suggests that the majority of 'deprived and powerless' parents will be able to become 'adequate' given 'the right sort of help' (p7). He points out however, that some parents will not accept this help and argues that workers and agencies need to re-establish authority and power in these instances.

In relation to staff White (1990) points out that the individual worker's (and particularly the social worker's legal authority is vested in their agencies), may often find themselves in powerless and isolated positions, despite being regarded by the family (and other disciplines) as powerful. White goes on to point out that power is usually 'accumulated ... and clung on to' by the management of an agency, and consequently employees are 'disabled' (p7). Gender may be of relevance in this analysis, as most managers are male and most workers are female (Allan et al, 1992; Lupton, 1992), and silencing is also an important factor (Nelson, 1997).

For children, White argues, empowerment is not sufficient. He cites the complaints procedures (in relation to section 26 of the Children Act 1989) as an example of a potentially damaging course of action. 'Complaints procedures are fine in theory as one method of helping children towards self-determination ... however, if they do no more than provide the child with an opportunity for making a complaint without real hope that his complaint will be heard and attended to, they may do more harm than good' (White, 1990, p8).

This, I feel is missing the point of 'empowerment', and is as relevant to adults (mothers, fathers, workers or whoever), as it is to children. Providing someone with opportunity is not the same as providing them with power, they must be able (or enabled) to seize the opportunity. Workers, and society generally, has to find ways of empowering non-abusing parents in a way which doesn't endanger children, nor disempower mothers. The Children Act 1989 and subsequent guidelines offer power indiscriminately by failing to distinguish between abusing and non-abusing parents, and between mothers and fathers. New working models need to be thought through before powers are withdrawn or granted.

The power imbalance between men and women continues to be a major factor in obstructing good practice. Many writers have acknowledged the particular connection between child sexual abuse, power and gender (Parton, 1989; Driver & Droisen, 1989; Herman, 1982; Russell, 1986; Dominelli, 1989). Unlike physical abuse and neglect, which may be regarded as relating to parenting (and therefore located in issues of socialisation, class and the gendered divisions of child care), sexual abuse has been regarded as a problem relating to male power and masculine socialisation (MacLeod & Saraga, 1988; Pringle, 1995; Cree & Cavanagh, 1996; Trotter et al, forthcoming).

The feminist analysis of child sexual abuse as a power relationship has provided a useful analysis of the position; that those of us in society with personal and structural power have an option to misuse it, and those who in addition operate from a personal power base which is rooted in fear and anger, are at greatest risk of becoming persecutors and child abusers. Such discussions about gender and power, seemed to have very little relevance on an individual level for the mothers and father in this book, yet the facts were unavoidable to me in overview. All ten children were abused by men. All ten had non-abusing mothers\mother-figures available to them but only four of them had non-abusing fathers\father-figures.

It is possible to see that although most men (and most fathers) possess personal and structural power, many of them do not operate from a base which is rooted in fear and anger, and therefore do not misuse their power by sexually abusing children. Furthermore, most women also possess some power (for example white women compared to black women, employed women compared to unemployed women, and all women compared to children), but it is qualitatively less power than men, and less likely to be rooted or socialised in anger and aggression (and therefore also less likely to result in the sexual abuse of children).

Hanmer's (1990) proposal that fathers and men gain a power advantage in society by not participating in childrearing processes is interesting, but without carefully examining the nature of the involvement, or scrutinising the gender\power imbalances in families, no meaningful conclusions, as to the actual powers fathers have in comparison to mothers (or to children), can be made.

As Fein (1978) suggested, men are seen to be important to children as symbols of power and authority, and this symbolic power and authority is often real when embodied by fathers. Clearly power is not always a negative quality and fathers (and mothers) can and do use it to protect and guide their children. The mothers in this book were clearly able take control and be powerful when they felt it necessary. Edith successfully argued with professionals in defence of Darren, Susan felt as though she literally 'took' power from Matthew's abuser.

*.... Every time he hit my son I hit him back. I did exactly what he did to my son, I did it to him...... I was getting really.....really taking power on. (Susan)*

The power that abusers have and use over children and others (professionals as well as non-abusing parents), should not be underestimated. Susan's experience (above) was not how she always felt, and many of the other mothers expressed their powerlessness in comparison to the abusers. All the parents described some of these feelings, the dynamics have many parallels with those experienced by victims: their territory and their child's body space have been invaded against their will; they and\or their children are coerced or manipulated by the abuser; they and\or their children are thwarted in their attempts to prevent further abuse or secure retribution (Finkelhor, 1986).

Hooper (1992) emphasises that it is important for workers not to assume that because powerlessness is an issue in common for women and children in a patriarchal society, and in abusive situations, they are not necessarily equal in their powerlessness nor have interests in common. Nor should it be assumed that powerlessness is static, non-abusing mothers and fathers' positions can change. Practitioners need to be alert to the different, individual sources of power in children, non-abusing and abusing mothers and fathers, and respond accordingly, maximising the power of the children and the non-abusing parents and minimising the power of the abusers.

One of the most effective ways which professionals could achieve this would be by reducing and sharing some of their own power. An acknowledgement and respect for the work undertaken by survivors and survivors' groups would be an excellent place to start. By providing support and valuing such work, professionals would also reduce some of the power held by abusers, much of which relies on the 'rubbishing' and minimising of survivors' accounts and perspectives. Jane, Astrid, Susan and Mary all found great support and strength from survivors' groups and Mary felt particularly appreciative.

> *One of the interesting things I found from the women's group was that a lot of them said that if they hadn't known me first they wouldn't have let me into the group, because a lot of them'd had rejection from their mothers. It's given them a different perspective, and they feel well its nice to know there's some mothers out there that are not like that. They get something from me as well as me getting something from them. (Mary).*

## A New Approach

According to the Central Council for Education and Training in Social Work (1991) all newly qualified social workers should be expected to hold a belief in the value of '... empowering all parents and carers to fulfil their parental responsibilities while recognizing the lack of power experienced by many mothers and female carers'. (p32). Further on the Council suggests that newly

## Implications for Practice

qualified social workers should be alert to the importance of the father's role, to involving him and 'of avoiding gender stereotyping' (p36). These are crucial issues for the future.

Gender stereotyping for the mothers and father in this study may have had effects which are difficult to pinpoint. It is impossible to know whether or not the workers involved with the parents were guilty of gender stereotyping, nor to what extent the parents themselves were influenced by assumptions about the gender of workers. Four of the mothers felt they were left to get on with things as though, perhaps, it was assumed that as mothers they would have natural coping instincts.

*How can I help him, ... I don't know how to do it? I'm only going by mother instinct. I could be doing more damage than anything, I don't know. (Edith)*

Susan, who expressed her anger and frustration violently (not a socially acceptable way for females), may have been perceived in psychopathological terms by professionals, who seemed to distrust her opinions and ignore her views. Susan doubted herself and her 'sanity', and had repeatedly questioned her own worth as a woman.

*I keep punishing myself for something that isn't my fault ... I was abused five times, including by my mother ... I take fits and I'm violent ... I fractured three of her ribs, and blacked her eye ... it took four doctors to get us off her ... they said I was like the hulk ... I've got really screwed up. (Susan)*

As Hooper (1989) emphasised, workers should help to build self-esteem of mothers as well as helping to mobilize support networks and giving practical help. A focus on self-esteem may have crucial implications for fathers as well as for mothers. Taking her analysis further, workers (undertaking longer-term support work with parents) who attempt to reinforce performances which match stereotyped or traditional roles for fathers and mothers, may:

a. for mothers result in feelings of guilt (about the bits of their lives which provide them with experiences of autonomy or self-worth), and cause depression or other mental health problems and decreased self-esteem;
b. for fathers result in feelings of alienation (about the bits of

their lives which provide them with experiences of nurturing or caring), and cause aggression or withdrawal and decreased self-esteem.

'On a broader level, anything that reduces women's dependence on marriage for their sense of identity and economic survival will increase their ability to act decisively to protect their children from violent partners. Current directions in social policy which reinforce women's dependency and emphasise women's traditional family responsibilities can only make this more difficult'. (Hooper, 1989, p29). Similarly then, anything which reinforces men's dependence on activities outside the family (work, sport, and so on) for their sense of identity and self-worth will decrease their ability to act supportively and caringly towards their children and partners.

Building self-esteem, increasing independence and self-reliance appear to be key elements for reducing gender stereotyping for both mothers and fathers, for increasing mother's power and, in the longer term, for protecting children.

It is likely that some parents will abuse their powers (as will some professionals), and as I have mentioned earlier, there is a potentially greater danger in giving any additional power to men in an already patriarchal society. It may be possible, however, to envisage a child protection system which has a non-patriarchal structure. In order to empower children, adults must relinquish some of their power. Similarly, in order to empower women, men must relinquish some of their power and in order for clients to be empowered, professionals must relinquish power.

Adults might disencumber themselves of some of the trappings of adulthood by adjusting their language, manner and appearance to be more approachable and understandable to children. Professionals might share some of their power with parents, at case conferences for example, by reducing the numbers who attend. Male managers could step aside so that women workers can take power in the positions that attract higher salaries and higher status. Men workers might involve themselves at more grass-roots levels, sanctioned by female management. However, given the increasing awareness of abuse by professionals when children are removed from home (Pringle, 1992), we might be better served harnessing the resources of women rather than increasing men's access to children.

Workers must include fathers in their work as a matter of

course. They could begin by seeking fathers' opinions and views on all matters and at all stages of the work, whilst always consulting mothers and collaborating with survivors.

As mentioned earlier, Mary found that women survivors were immensely helpful to her and to Caroline, despite their initial reservations about helping a 'mother'.

If power imbalances and prejudicial stereotypes could be minimised, in order that practitioners and clients could work together on a more equal basis, a new approach to the management, treatment and prevention of child sexual abuse might be achievable.

This book has attempted to present some new ideas about non-abusing parents, and with the cooperation and assistance of the mothers and fathers, has developed a new perspective. The capacity of non-abusing mothers and fathers to love, protect and care for their children appears to be extensive; the recognition of this may yet prove to be the most important factor for workers to address in the future.

# References

Abbott, F. (ed) (1990) *Men and Intimacy.* Freedom, Ca.: The Crossing Press

Abel, G.G., Becker, J.V., Cunningham-Rathner, J., Mittelman, M. & Rouleau, J.L. (1988) *Multiple Paraphilic Diagnoses Among Sex Offenders.* Bulletin of American Academical Psychiatry and Law.

Adams-Tucker, C. (1982) 'Proximate effects of sexual abuse in childhood' *American Journal of Psychiatry,* 139, 1252-1256.

Adams-Tucker, C. (1986) 'Defense Mechanisms used by Sexually Abused Children' in Haden, D.C. (ed) *Out of Harm's Way,* Phoenix, Az.: Oryx Press.

Adcock, M., White, R. & Hollows, A. (1991) Child Protection. A training and practice resource pack for work under the Children Act 1989. Londn: National Children's Bureau.

Ahmad, B. (1989) 'Child care and ethnic minorities' in Kahan, B. (ed) *Child Care Research, Policy and Practice,* London: Hodder and Stoughton.

Allan, M., Bhavani, R. & French, K. (1992) *Promoting Women,* London: Social Services Inspectorate\HMSO.

Ash, A. (1984) *Father-Daughter Sexual Abuse: the Abuse of Paternal Authority,* Bangor: Dept. of Social Theory and Institutions, Univ. College of N. Wales.

Backett, K.C. (1982) *Mothers and Fathers: A Study of the Development and Negotiation of Parental Behaviour.* London: Macmillan Press.

Baker, A.W. & Duncan, S.P. (1985) 'Child sexual abuse: a study of prevalence in Great Britain', *Child Abuse and Neglect,* 9, 457-67.

Bannister, A. (ed) (1992) *From Hearing to Healing.* Harlow: Longman.

Barker, R.W. (1994) *Lone Fathers and Masculinities*, Aldershot: Avebury.

Bass, E. & Davis, L. (1988) *The Courage to Heal.* New York: Harper & Row.

Bennetts, C., Brown, M. & Sloan, J. (1992) *AIDS, the Hidden Agenda in Child Sexual Abuse.* Harlow: Longman.

Berliner, L. (1991a) 'Interviewing Families', in Murray K & Gough D A (eds) *Interviewing in Child Sexual Abuse.* Edinburgh: Scottish Academic Press.

Berliner, L. (1991b) 'Therapy with Victimized Children and their Families', *New Directions for Mental Health Services,* 51, 29-46.

Bigner, J.J. & Jacobsen, R.B. (1992) 'Adult Responses to Child Behavior and Attitudes Towards Fathering: Gay and Nongay Fathers', *Journal of Homosexuality* 23(3), 99-112.

Biller, H. (1974) *Paternal Deprivation,* Lexington: D.C.Heath.

Birchall, E. (1995) *Working Together in Child Protection*, London: HMSO.

Blume, E.S. (1990) *Secret Survivors. Uncovering Incest and Its Aftereffects in Women,* Chichester: Wiley.

Booth, A. & Edwards, J.N. (1980) 'Fathers: The Invisible Parent', *Sex Roles,* 6, 445-56.

Booth, T. & Booth, W. (1994) *Parenting Under Pressure: mothers and fathers with learning difficulties,* Buckingham: Open University.

Bowlby, J. (1965) *Child Care and the Growth of Love,* Harmondsworth: Penguin.

Bowlby, J. (1969) *Attachment and loss: Vol 1,* London: Hogarth Press.

Bray, M. (1991) *Poppies on the Rubbish Heap. Sexual Abuse The Child's Voice,*

## References

Edinburgh: Canongate Press.

Breakwell, G. (1986) *Coping with Threatened Identities*, London: Methuen.

Brod, H. (ed) (1987) *The Making of Masculinities: The New Men's Sudies*, London: Allen and Unwin.

Brown, A. (1982) 'Fathers in the labour ward: Medical and lay accounts', in McKee, L. & O'Brien, M. (eds) *The Father Figure*, London: Tavistock.

Brown, C. (1989) *Child Abuse Parents Speaking: Parents Impressions of Social Workers and the Social Work Process*, Bristol: SAUS, Working Paper 63.

Burgess, A.W., Hartman, C.R., McCausland, M.P. & Powers, P. (1984) *Impact of Child Pornography and Sex Rings on Child Victims and Their Families*, in Burgess, A.W. (ed) *Child Pornography and Sex Rings*, New York: Lexington Books.

Burgess, A.W. (1975) 'Family Reaction to Homicide', *American Journal of Orthopsychiatry*, 45(3), 391-398

Burgess, A.W., Hartman, C.R., McCauslan, M.P. & Powers, P. (1984) 'Response Patterns in Children and Adolescents Exploited Through Sex Rings and Pornography', *American Journal of Psychiatry*, 141:5, 656-662

Butler, I. & Williamson, H. (1994) *Children Speak: Children, Trauma and Social Work*, Harlow, Essex: Longman.

Butler, S. & Willott, C. (1993) 'Untapped Power: Life Pattern Work as a Tool for Change in the Lives of Women Survivors of Childhood Sexual Abuse', in Ferguson, H., Gilligan, R. & Torode, R. (eds) *Surviving Childhood Adversity: Issues for Policy and Practice*, Dublin: Social Studies Press.

Byerly, C.M. (1985) *The Mother's Book. How to Survive the Incest of Your Child*, Dubuque, Iowa: Kendall\Hunt.

Campbell, B. (1993) *Goliath. Britain's Dangerous Places*, London: Methuen.

Campbell, B. (1988) *Unofficial Secrets: Child Sexual Abuse: The Cleveland Case*, London: Virago.

Campion, M.J. (1995) *Who's Fit to be a Parent*, London: Routledge.

Canaan, J.E. & Griffin, C. (1990) 'The new men's studies: part of the problem or part of the solution?' in Hearn, J. & Morgan, D. (eds) *Men, Masculinities and Social Theory*, London: Unwin Hyman.

Cashman, H. (1993) *Christianity and child sexual abuse*, London: Society for Promoting Christian Knowledge.

Cashman, H. & Lamballe-Armstrong, A. (1991) 'The Unwanted Message: Child Protection Through Community Awareness' in Richardson, S. & Bacon, H. *Child Sexual Abuse: Whose Problem?* Birmingham: Venture Press.

Cavanagh, K. & Cree, V.E. (eds) (1996) *Working With Men: Feminism and Social Work*, London: Routledge.

CCETSW (1991) *The Teaching of Child Care in the Diploma in Social Work*, London: Central Council for Education and Training in Social Work.

Chodorow, N. (1978) *The Reproduction of Mothering*, Berkely: University of California Press.

Cleaver, H. & Freeman, P. (1995) *Parental Perspectives in Cases of Suspected Child Abuse*, London: HMSO.

Cloke, C. & Davies, M. (eds) (1995) *Participation and Empowerment in Child Protection*, London: Pitman.

Collier, R. (1995) *Masculinity, Law and the Family*, London: Routledge.

Cohn, A.H. & Daro, D. (1987) 'Is treatment too late? What ten years of evaluative research tell us', *Child Abuse and Neglect*, 11, 433-42.

Coltrane, S. (1988) 'Father-Child Relationships and the Status of Women: A

Cross-Cultural Study', *American Journal of Sociology* 93(5), 1060-95

Coohey, C. (1996) 'Child Maltreatment: Testing the Social Isolation Hypothesis', *Child Abuse & Neglect*, 20(3), 241-254.

Cook, J.A. (1988) 'Dad's Double Binds. Rethinking Fathers' Bereavement from a Men's Studies Perspective', *Journal of Contemporary Ethnography*, 17(3), 285-308.

Cooper, D.M. (1993) *Child Abuse Revisited. Children, Society and Social Work*, Buckingham: Open University Press.

Corby, B. (1987) 'Why ignoring the rights of parents in child abuse cases should be avoided', *Social Work Today*, 19(13), 8-9.

Cox, P. (1993) 'Professional Survival - a Double Jeopardy: Some Implications for Training, Education and Practice', in Ferguson, H., Gilligan, R. & Torode, R. (eds) *Surviving Childhood Adversity: Issues for Policy and Practice*, Dublin: Social Studies Press.

Craig, E., Erooga, M., Morrison, T. & Shearer, E. (1989) 'Making sense of Sexual Abuse - charting the shifting sands', in NSPCC *Child Sexual Abuse*, Harlow: Longman.

Cree, V.E. & Cavanagh, K. (1996) 'Men, masculinism and social work', in Cavanagh, K. & Cree, V.E. (eds) *Working With Men: Feminism and Social Work*, London: Routledge.

Crompton, M. (1990) *Attending to Children: Direct work in social and health care*, London: Edward Arnold.

Danica, E. (1989) *don't. a woman's word*, London: The Women's Press.

Davis, E., Kidd, L. & Pringle, K. (1987) *Child Sexual Abuse Training Programme for Foster Parents with Teenage Placements*, Newcastle: Barnardo's.

Deblinger, E., Hathaway, C.R., Lippmann, J. & Steer, R. (1993) 'Psychosocial Characteristics and Correlates of Symptom Distress in Nonoffending Mothers of Sexually Abused Children', *Journal of Interpersonal Violence*, 8(2), 155-168

De Jong, A. (1988) 'Maternal Responses to the Sexual Abuse of Their Children', *Pediatrics*, 81(1)

Department of Health (1988) *Protecting Children: A Guide for Social Workers Undertaking a Comprehensive Assessment*, London: HMSO.

Department of Health (1989a), The Children Act 1989, London: HMSO.

Department of Health (1989b) *An Introduction to the Children Act 1989*, London: HMSO.

Department of Health (1991a) *Child Abuse: A study of inquiry reports 1980 - 1989*, London: HMSO.

Department of Health (1991b) *The Children Act 1989 Guidance and Regulations Volume 3: Family Placements*, London: HMSO.

Department of Health (1995) *The Challenge of Partnership in Child Protection: Practice Guide*, London: Social Services Inspectorate/HMSO.

DHSS & Welsh Office (1988) *Working Together: A Guide to Inter-agency Co-operation for the Protection of children from Abuse*, London: HMSO.

Dibblin, J. (1987) 'The right of the father?' *New Statesman*, 10 July.

Dienhart, A. & Daly, K. (1997) 'Men and Women Cocreating Father Involvemnet in a Nongenerative Culture', in Hawkins, A.J. & Dollahite, D.C. (eds) *Generative Fathering: Beyond Deficit Perspectives*, London: Sage.

Dominelli, L. (1989) 'Betrayal of Trust: A Feminist Analysis of Power Relationships in Incest Abuse and its Relevance for Social Work Practice', *British Journal of Social Work*, 19, 291-307

Doughty, D.L. & Schneider, H.G. (1987) 'Attribution of Blame in Incest Among

## References

Mental Health Professionals', *Psychological Reports*, 60, 1159-1165

Driver, E. & Droisen, A. (1989) *Child Sexual Abuse. Feminist perspectives*, London: Macmillan.

Ehrensaft, D. (1992) 'Preschool Child Sexual Abuse: The aftermath of the Presidio Case', *American Journal of Orthopsychiatry*, 62, 234-244.

Eichenbaum, L. & Orbach, S. (1982) *Outside In ... Inside Out*, Harmondsworth: Penguin.

Elliott, M. (ed) (1993) *Female Sexual Abuse of Children: The ultimate taboo*, Harlow: Longman.

Everson, M.D., Hunter, W.M., Runyon, D.K., Edelsohn, G.A. & Coulter, M.L. (1989) 'Maternal Support Following Disclosure of Incest' *American Journal of Orthopsychiatry*, 59(2)

Faller, K.C. (1990) *Understanding Child Sexual Maltreatment*, London: Sage.

Farmer, E. & Owen, M. (1995) *Child Protection Practice: Private Risks and Public Remedies*, London: HMSO

Fawcett, B., Featherstone, B., Hearn, J. & Toft, C. (eds) (1996) *Violence and Gender Relations: Theories and Interventions*, London: Sage.

Featherstone, B. & Harlow, E. (1996) 'Organised Abuse: Themes and Issues', in Fawcett, B., Featherstone, B., Hearn, J. & Toft, C. (eds) *Violence and Gender Relations: Theories and Interventions*, London: Sage.

Fein, R.A. (1978) 'Research in Fathering: Social Policy and an Emergent Perspectice', *Journal of Social Issues*, 34

Finkelhor, D. (1984) *Child Sexual Abuse, New Theory and Research*, New York: The Free Press.

Finkelhor, D., Araji, S., Baron, L., Browne, A., Peters, S. D. & Wyatt, G. E. (1986) *A Sourcebook on Child Sexual Abuse*, London: Sage.

Finkelhor, D. (1991) 'The Lazy Revolutionary's Guide to the Prospects for Reforming Child Welfare', *Child Abuse and Neglect*, 15(sup 1), 17-23.

Finkelhor, D. & Browne, A. (1986) 'Initial and Long-Term Effects: A Conceptual Framework', in Finkelhor, D. and associates *A sourcebook on child sexual abuse*, London: Sage.

Finkelhor, D., Hotaling, G., Lewis, I.A. & Smith, C. (1990) 'Sexual Abuse in a National Survey of Adult Men and Women: Prevalence, Characteristics and Risk Factors', *Child Abuse and Neglect*, 14, 19-28.

Fisher, M., Marsh, P., Phillips, D. & Sainsbury, E. (1986) *In and Out of Care*, London: Batsford\BAAF.

Franklin, C.W. (1984) *The Changing Definition of Masculinity*, London: Plenum Press.

Fraser, S. (1987) *My Father's House*, London: Virago.

Frenken, J. & Van Stolk, B. (1990) 'Incest Victims: Inadequate Help by Professionals', *Child Abuse and Neglect*, 14, 253-263.

Friedrich, W.N. (1991) 'Mothers of Sexually Abused Children: an MMPI Study', *Journal of Clinical Psychology*, 47(6), 778-783.

Furniss, T. (1991) *The Multi Professional Handbook of Child Sexual Abuse: Integrated Maneagement, Therapy and Legal Intervention*, London: Routledge.

Garbarino, J. (1993) 'Reinventing Fatherhood', *Families in Society*, January 1993

Ghate, D. & Spencer, L. (1995) *The Prevalence of Child Sexual Abuse in Britain*, London: HMSO.

Giarretto, H. (1982) *Integrated Treatment of Child Sexual Abuse*, Palo Alto, Calif.: Science and Behaviour Books Inc.

Gillies, E. (1991) 'Parents United Programmes', in Murray, K. & Gough, D.A. (eds)

*Interviewing in Child Sexual Abuse*, Edinburgh: Scottish Academic Press.
Gomes-Schwartz, B., Horowitz, J.M. & Cardarelli, A.P. (1990) *Child Sexual Abuse: The Initial Effects*, London: Sage.
Gough, D. (1993) *Child Abuse Interventions: A review of the research literature*, London: HMSO.
Grabrucker, M. (1988) *There's a Good Girl: Gender Stereotyping in the First Three Years of Life*, London: The Women's Press.
Grant, F.J. (1992) *Child Sexual Abuse "The Silent Victims"*, Author's own publication.
Greif, G.L. & Zuravin, S.J. (1989) 'Fathers: A Placement Resource for Abused and Neglected Children?', *Child Welfare*, LXVIII(5), 479-490
Greif, G.L. (1985) *Single Fathers*, New York: Lexington Books.
Greif, G.L. & Bailey, C. (1990) 'Where are the Fathers in Social Work Literature?', *Families in Society*, February 1990, 88-92.
Greif, G.L. & DeMaris, A. (1990) 'Single Fathers with Custody', *Families in Society*, May 1990, 259-266.
Griggs, D.R. & Boldi, A. (1995) 'Parallel Treatment of Parents of Abuse Reactive Children', in Hunter, M. (ed) *Child Survivors and Perpetrators of Sexual Abuse: Treatment Innovations*, London: Sage.
Grossman, F.K., Pollack, W.S. & Golding, E. (1988) 'Fathers and Children:- Predicting the Quality and Quantity of Fathering', *Developmental Psychology*, 24(1), 82-91.
Hall, L. & Lloyd, S. (1989) *Surviving Child Sexual Abuse: A Handbook for Helping Women Change Their Past*, London: Falmer Press.
Hallett, C. (1995) *Inter-agency Coordination and Child Protection*, London: HMSO.
Ham, J.B. (1985) 'Common Religious Issues Surrounding Incest', in Byerly, C.M. *The Mother's Book. How to survive the Incest of Your Child*, Dubuque, Iowa: Kendall\Hunt.
Hanmer, J. (1990) 'Men, power and the exploitation of women', in Hearn, J. & Morgan, D. (eds) *Men, Masculinities and Social Theory*, London: Allen & Unwin.
Hanmer, J. & Maynard, M. (eds) (1987) *Women, Violence and Social Control*, London: Macmillan.
Harding, L.F. (1991) *Perspectives in Child Care Policy*, Harlow: Longman.
Harris, K.M. & Morgan, S.P. (1991) 'Fathers, Sons, and Daughters: Differential Paternal Involvement in Parenting', *Journal of Marriage and the Family*, 53, 531-544.
Hawkes, C., Jenkins, J.A. & Vizard, E. (1997) 'Roots of Sexual Violence in Children and Adolescents' in Varma, V. (ed) *Violence in Children and Adolescents*, London: Jessica Kingsley.
Hawkins, A.J., Christiansen, S.L., Sargent, K.P. & Hill, E.J. (1995) 'Rethinking Fathers' Involvement in Child Care: A Developmental Perspective', in Marsiglio, W. (ed) *Fatherhood: Contemporary Theory, Research, and Social Policy*, London: Sage.
Hawkins, A.J. & Dollahite, D.C. (eds) (1997) *Generative Fathering: Beyond Deficit Perspectives*, London: Sage.
Hearn, J. & Morgan, D. (1990) *Men, Masculinities and Social Theory*, London: Unwin Hyman.
Hedley, R. & Dorkeno, E. (1992) *Child Protection and Female Genital Mutilation. Advice for Health, Education, and Social Work Professionals*, London: Forward.
Herman, J. (1982) *Father-daughter incest*, Cambridge, Mass.: Harvard University

# References

Press.

Herzog, E. & Saudia, C. (1974) 'Children in Fatherless Families', in Hetherington, E.M. & Riccicuti, P. (eds) *Review of Child Development Research, Volume 3*, Chicago: Chicago University Press.

Hetherington, E.M. & Riccicuti, P. (eds) (1974) *Review of Child Development Research, Volume 3*, Chicago: Chicago University Press.

Hirst, G. & Cox, P. (1996) 'Hearing all sides of the story: the challenge of integrating teaching on sexual aggression into social work qualifying training', *Journal of Sexual Aggression*, 2(1), 33-48.

HMSO (1989) *An Introduction to The Children Act*, London: HMSO.

HMSO (1985) *Social Work Decisions in Child Care*, London: HMSO.

Hooper, C-A. (1992) *Mothers Surviving Child Sexual Abuse*, London: Routledge.

Hooper, C-A. (1989) 'Alternatives to Collusion: the Response of Mothers to Child Sexual Abuse in the Family', *Educational and Child Psychology*, 6(1), 22-30.

Hooper, C-A. & Humphreys, C. (1997) 'What's in a Name? Reflections on the Term 'Non-Abusing Parent'', *Child Abuse Review*, 6, 298-303.

Hudson, A. (1989) 'Changing perspectives: feminism, gender and social work', in Langan, M. & Lee, P. *Radical Social Work Today*, London: Unwin Hyman.

Hunter, M. (ed) (1995) *Child Survivos and Perpetrators of Sexual Abuse: Treatment Innovations*, London: Sage.

Jackson, V. (1996) *Racism and Child Protection: The Black Experience of Child Sexual Abuse*, London: Cassell.

Johnson, J.T. (1992) *Mothers of Incest Survivors*, Bloomington, Ind.: Indiana University Press.

Kahan, B. (ed) (1989) *Child Care Research, Policy and Practice*, London: Hodder & Stoughton.

Katz, I. (1995) 'Approaches to empowerment and participation in child protection', in Cloke, C. & Davies, M. (eds) *Participation and Empowerment in Child Protection*, London: Pitman.

Kelly, L. (1987) 'The continuum of sexual violence', in Hanmer, J. & Maynard, M. (eds) *Women, Violence and Social Control*, London: Macmillan.

Kelly, L. (1988) *Surviving Sexual Violence*, Cambridge: Polity.

Kelly, L. (1993) 'Organised sexual abuse: What do we know and what do we need to know?', in Child Abuse Studies Unit (ed) *Abuse of Women and Children: A Feminist Response*, London: University of North London Press.

Kennedy, G.E. (1989) 'Involving Students in Participatory Research on Fatherhood: A Case Study', *Family Relations*, 38, 363-370.

Kennedy, M. (1992) 'Not the Only Way to Communicate: A Challenge to Voice in Child Protection Work', *Child Abuse Review*, 1, 169-177.

Klein, M. (1959) 'Our Adult World and its Roots in Infancy', in Klein, M. (1988) *Envy and Gratitude and Other Works 1946-1963*, London: Virago.

Kikuchi, J.J. (1995) 'When the Offender is a Child: Identifying and Responding to Juvenile Sexual Abuse', in Hunter, M. (ed) *Child Survivors and Perpetrators of Sexual Abuse: Treatment Innovations*, London: Sage.

King, M.B. (1995) 'Parents who are gay or lesbian', in Reder, P. & Lucey, C. (eds) *Assessment of Parenting*, London: Routledge.

Kitzinger, J. (1996) 'Media Representations of Sexual Abuse Risks', *Child Abuse Review*, 5, 319-333

Kitzinger, J. (1997) 'Who are you kidding?', in James, A. & Prout, A. (eds) *Constructing and Reconstructing Childhood, Second Edition*, London: Falmer Press.

La Fontaine, J. (1990) *Child Sexual Abuse,* Cambridge: Polity.
Lamb, M.E. (1981) *The Role of the Father in Child Development,* Chichester: Wiley.
Lamb, M.E. (ed) (1986) *The Father's Role: Applied Perspectives,* Chichester: Wiley.
Langan, M. & Day, L. (1992) *Women, Oppression & Social Work,* London: Routledge.
Langan, M. & Lee, P. (1989) *Radical Social Work Today,* London: Unwin Hyman.
Lanning, K.V. & Burgess, A.W. (1984) 'Child Pornography and Sex Rings', *FBI Law Enforcement Bulletin,* January 1984, 10-16.
Levine, J.A. (1993) 'Involving Fathers in Head Start: A Framework for Public Policy and Program Development', *Families in Society,* 74(1) 4-19.
Levitt, C.J., Owen, G. & Truchsess, J. (1991) 'Families After Sexual Abuse: What Helps? What is Needed?', in Patton, M.Q. (ed) *Family Sexual Abuse,* London: Sage.
Levy, A. & Kahan, B. (1991) *The Pindown Experience and the Protection of Children. The report of the Staffordshire Child Care Inquiry 1990,* Staffordshire County Council.
Lew, M. (1990) *Victims No Longer. Men Recovering from Incest and Other Sexual Child Abuse,* New York: Harper Perennial.
Lisak, D. (1991) 'Sexual aggression, masculinity and fathers', *Signs,* Winter, 238-262.
Logan, J., Kershaw, S., Karban, K., Mills, S., Trotter, J. & Sinclair, M. (1996) *Confronting Prejudice: Lesbian and Gay Isuues in Social Work Education,* Hampshire: Arena.
Lowe, N.V. (1982) 'The legal status of fathers: Past and present' in McKee, L. & O'Brien, M. (eds) *The Father Figure,* London: Tavistock.
London Borough of Greenwich (1987) *A Child in Mind: protection of Children in a Responsible Society: Report of the Commission of Inquiry into the Circumstances Surrounding the Death of Kimberley Carlile,* London Borough of Greenwich.
Lummis, T. (1982) 'The historical dimension of fatherhood: A case study 1890 - 1914' in McKee, L. & O'Brien, M. (eds) *The Father Figure,* London: Tavistock.
Lupton, C. (1992) 'Feminism, managerialism and performance measurement' in Langan, M. & Day, L. *Women, Oppression & Social Work,* London: Routledge.
MacFarlane, K. (1986) 'Helpin parents cope with extrafamilial molestation', in MacFarlane, K. & Waterman, J. (eds) *Sexual Abuse of Young Children,* London: Holt, Rinehart and Winston.
MacFarlane, K. & Waterman, J. (eds) (1986) *Sexual Abuse of Young Children,* London: Holt, Rinehart and Winston.
MacLeod, M. & Saraga, E. (1988) 'Challenging the Orthodoxy: Towards a Feminist Theory and Practice', *Feminist Review, Special Issue: Family Secrets. Child Sexual Abuse,* 28(Spring), 16-55.
MacLeod, M. & Saraga, E. (1991) 'Clearing a path through the undergrowth: a feminist reading of recent literature on child sexual abuse', in Carter, P., Jeffs, T. & Smith, M. (eds) *Social Work and Social Welfare Year Book 3,* Buckingham: Open University.
Maltz, W. & Holman, B. (1987) *Incest and sexuality: A Guide to Understanding and Healing,* New York: Lexington Books.
Manion, I.G., McIntyre, J., Firestone, P., Ligezinska, M., Ensom, R. & Wells, G. (1996) 'Secondary Traumatization in Parents Following the Disclosure of Extrafamilial Child Sexual Abuse: Initial Effects', *Child Abuse & Neglect,* 20(11), 1095-1109.

*References*

Margolin, L. (1992) 'Sexual Abuse by Grandparents', *Child Abuse and Neglect,* 16, 735-741.

Marsh, P. (1991) 'Social Work with Fathers', in Family Rights Group *The Children Act 1989: Working in Partnership with Families,* London: HMSO

Martin, J. (1983) 'Maternal and Paternal Abuse of Children. Theoretical and Research Perspectives', in Finkelhor, D. (ed) *The Dark Side of Families,* London: Sage.

Mattinson, J. & Sinclair, I. (1979) *Mate and Stalemate,* Oxford: Blackwell.

Mayer, J.E. & Timms, N. (1970) *The Client Speaks. Working class impressions of casework,* London & Henley: Routledge & Kegan Paul.

McFadden, E.J. (1984) *Preventing Abuse in Foster Care,* Eastern Michigan University.

McFadden, E.J. & Ryan, P. (1991) 'Maltreatment in Family Foster Homes: Dynamics And Dimensions', *Child and Youth Services,* 15(2)

McGloin, P. & Turnbull, A. (1987a) 'Strengthening good practice by bringing in the parents' *Social Work Today,* 18(46), 14-15.

McGloin, P. & Turnbull, A. (1987b) 'Child abuse reviews - the impact of the parents', *Social Work Today,* 19(6), 16-17.

McHugh, J. (ed) (1987) *Creative Social Work With Families,* Birmingham: British Association of Social Workers.

McKee, L. (1982) 'Fathers' participation in infant care: A critique', in McKee, L. & O'Brien, M. (eds) *The Father Figure,* London: Tavistock.

McKee, L. & O'Brien, M. (eds) (1982) *The Father Figure,* London: Tavistock.

Mendel, M.P. (1995) *The Male Survivor: The Impact of Sexual Abuse,* London: Sage.

Miller, A. (1985) *Thou Shalt Not Be Aware: Societies Betrayal of the Child,* London: Pluto Press.

Milner, J. (1992) 'Disappearing Fathers: The gendered nature of child protection interventions and the child protection systems in England', Unpublished paper given at *Surviving Childhood Adversity* conference: Trinity College, Dublin, July 1992

Milner, J. (1994) 'Men's Resistance to Social Workers', in Featherstone, B., Fawcett, B. & Toft, C. (eds) *Violence, Gender and Social Work,* Bradford: University of Bradford.

Milner, J. & Kelly, N. (1996) 'Child Protection Decision-Making', *Child Abuse Review,* 5, 91-102.

Monck, E. (1997) 'Evaluating Therapeutic Intervention with Sexually Abused Children', *Child Abuse Review,* 6, 163-177.

Morrison, P. (1991) 'Pregnant Fatherhood - 2 years on', in Seidler, V.J. (ed) *Men, Sexual Politics & Socialism,* London: Routledge.

Mostyn, Lord Williams of (1996) *Childhood Matters: Report of the National Commission of Inquiry into the Prevention of Child Abuse, Volume 2. Background Papers,* London: HMSO.

Murray, K. & Gough, D.A. (1991) *Interviewing in Child Sexual Abuse,* Edinburgh: Scottish Academic Press.

Myer, M.H. (1984) 'A New Look at Mothers of Incest Victims', *Journal of Social Work and Human Sexuality,* 3, 47-58.

Nelson, S. (1997) *Challenges for the Future,* Keynote paper for the Baspcan Third National Conference, Heriot-Watt University, Edinburgh, July 1997.

NSPCC (1989) *Child Sexual Abuse,* Harlow: Longman.

O'Hagan, K. (1997) 'The problem of engaging men in child protection work', *British*

Journal of Social Work, 27, 25-42.
Packman, J., Randall, J. & Jacques, N. (1986) *Who Needs Care? Social Work Decisions About Children,* Oxford: Basil Blackwell.
Packman, J. (1989) 'Decisions in child care', in Kahan, B. (ed) *Child Care Research, Policy and Practice,* London: Hodder and Stoughton.
Packman, J. & Randall, J. (1989) 'Decisions about children at risk', in Philpot, T. & Stills, P. (eds) *Current Challenges for Child Care and the Management of Child Abuse,* London Boroughs Training Committee and Community Care.
Palkovitz, R. (1997) 'Reconstructing "Involvement": Expanding Conceptualizations of Mens' Caring in Contemporary Families', in Hawkins, A.J. & Dollahite, D.C. (eds) *Generative Fathering: Beyond Deficit Perspectives,* London: Sage.
Palm, G.F. & Palkovitz, R. (1988) 'The Challenge of Working with New Fathers: Implications for Support Providers', *Marriage & Family Reviews,* 12(3-4), 357-76.
Parker, R., Ward, H., Jackson, S., Aldgate, J. & Wedge, P. (1991) *Assessing Outcomes in Child Care,* London: HMSO.
Parton, N. (1989) 'Child Abuse', in Kahan, B. *Child Care Research, Policy and Practice,* London: Hodder & Stoughton.
Parton, N. (1991) *Governing the Family,* London: Macmillan.
Parton, N., Thorpe, D. & Wattam, C. (1997) *Child Protection: Risk and the Moral Order,* London: Macmillan.
Pattison, C. (1992) 'Child Sexual Abuse - Integrating Work with Victims, their Families and Perpetrators', *Child Abuse Review,* 5(3), 16-19
Patton, M.Q. (1991) *Family Sexual Abuse. Frontline Research and Evaluation,* London: Sage.
Perlman, H.H. (1957) *Social Casework: A Problem Solving Process,* Chicago: University of Chicago Press.
Porter, R. (ed) (1984) *Child Sexual Abuse Within the Family,* London: Tavistock\CIBA Foundation.
Pringle, K. (1992) 'Gender Issues in the Sexual Abuse of Children by Welfare Professionals', Unpublished paper given at *Surviving Childhood Adversity* conference: Trinity College, Dublin, July 1992.
Pringle, K. (1993) 'Child sexual abuse perpetrated by welfare personnel and the problem of men', *Critical Social Policy,* 36, 4-19.
Pringle, K. (1995) *Men, Masculinities & Social Welfare,* London: UCL Press.
Pugh, G. & De'Ath, E. (1984) *The Needs of Parents. Practice and Policy in Parent Education,* London: Macmillan.
Reason, P. (ed) (1988) *Human Inquiry in Action. Developments in New Paradigm Research,* London: Sage.
Regehr, C. (1990) 'Parental Responses to Extrafamilial Child Sexual Assault', *Child Abuse and Neglect,* 14, 113-120.
Remy, J. (1990) 'Patriarchy and fratriarchy as forms of androcracy', in Hearn, J. & Morgan, D. (eds) *Men, Masculinities and Social Theory,* London: Unwin Hyman.
Renvoize, J. (1993) *Innocence Destroyed: a study of child sexual abuse,* London: Routledge.
Richards, M.P.M. (1982) 'How should we approach the study of fathers?', in McKee, L. & O'Brien, M. (eds) *The Father Figure,* London: Tavistock.
Richardson, S. & Bacon, H. (eds) (1991) *Child Sexual Abuse: Whose Problem?,* Birmingham: Venture Press.
Richman, J. & Goldthorpe, W.O. (1978) 'Fatherhood: The Social Construction of

## References

Pregnancy and Birth', in Kitzinger, S. & Davis, J. (eds) *The Place of Birth*, Oxford: Oxford University Press.

Richman, J. (1982) 'Men's experiences of pregnancy and chldbirth' in McKee, L. & O'Brien, M. (eds) *The Father Figure*, London: Tavistock.

Rogers, C.R. (1951) *Client Centred Therapy*, London: Constable.

Rogers, W.S., Roche, J. & Dickenson, D. (1991) *The Children Act 1989: Putting it into Practice. Focus on Practice Workbook*, Buckingham: Open University.

Russell, D.E.H. (1986) *The Secret Trauma: Incest in the lives of girls and women*, Basic Books.

ref>Sackett, V.A. (1988) 'Daddy's Dearest', *Public Opinion*, March\April, 18

Sanderson, C. (1990) *Counselling Adult Survivors of Child Sexual Abuse*, London: Jessica Kingsley.

Segal, L. (1990) *Slow Motion: Changing Masculinities, Changing Men*, London: Virago.

Seidler, V.J. (ed) (1991) *Men, Sexual Politics & Socialism*, London: Routledge.

Sgroi, S. & Dana, N. (1982) 'Individual and group treatment of mothers of incest victims', in Sgroi, S. (ed) *Handbook of Clinical Intervention in Child Sexual Abuse*, New York: Lexington Books.

Sgroi, S. (ed) (1982) *Handbook of Clinical Intervention in Child Sexual Abuse*, New York: Lexington Books.

Sharland, E., Jones, D., Aldgate, J., Seal, H. & Croucher, M. (1995) *Professional Intervention in Child Sexual Abuse*, London: HMSO

Smith, K. & Breathwick, P. (1987) 'Family Resource Centres and Family Breakdown', in McHugh, J. (ed) *Creative Social Work With Families*, Birmingham: British Association of Social Workers.

Stark, E. & Flitcraft, A.H. (1988), 'Women and children at risk: a feminist perspective on child abuse', *International Journal of Health Services*, 18, 97-118.

Staunton, D.D.L. & Darling, N. (1992) 'Group Work with Mothers of Sexually Abused Children - Participant Observation', Unpublished paper given at *Surviving Childhood Adversity* conference: Trinity College, Dublin, July 1992

Stephanie Fox Review Panel (1990) *The Report of the Stephanie Fox Practice Review*, Wandsworth Area Child Protection Committee.

Stevenson, O. (1989) 'Multi-disciplinary work in child protection', in Kahan, B. *Child Abuse. Public Policy and Professional Practice*, Brighton: Harvester Wheatsheaf.

Stevenson, O. (1991) 'Preface', in CCETSW (ed) *The Teaching of Child Care in the Diploma in Social Work*, London: Central Council for Education and Training in Social Work.

Strand, V.C. (1991) 'Mid-phase Treatment with Mothers in Incest Families', *Clinical Social Work Journal*, 19(4), 377-389.

Stroh, G.M. (1995) 'Ritual Abuse: Traumas and Treatment', in Hunter, M. (ed) *Child Survivors and Perpetrators of Sexual Abuse: Treatment Innovations*, London: Sage.

Stubbs, P. (1989) 'Developing anti-racist practice - problems and possibilities', in NSPCC (ed) *Child Sexual Abuse*, Harlow: Longman.

Summit, R. (1983) 'The child sexual abuse accomodation syndrome', *Child Abuse and Neglect*, 7, 177-193.

Tasker, F.L. & Golombok, S. (1997) *Growing Up in a Lesbian Family: Effects on Child Development*, London: Guildford Press.

Tate, T. (1991) *Children for the Devil. Ritual abuse and satanic crime*, London: Methuan.

Taylor, G. (1993) 'Challenges from the Margins', in Clarke, J. (ed) *A Crisis in Care? Challenges to Social Work*, London: Sage.

Taylor-Browne, J. (1997) 'Obfuscating Child Sexual Abuse II: Listening to Survivors', *Child Abuse Review*, 6, 118-127.

Thoburn, J., Lewis, A. & Shemmings, D. (1995) *Paternalism or Partnership? Family Involvement in the Child Protection Process*, London: HMSO.

Timms, R.J. & Connors, P. (1990) 'Sexual Abuse of Young Males: Removing the Secret', in Abbott, F. (ed) *Men and Intimacy*, Freedom, Ca.: The Crossing Press.

Trotter, J. (1993) 'Non-Abusing Fathers - Where are They?', Unpublished paper given at University of Huddersfield 21.10.93

Trotter, J. (1991) 'Wanting Protection', *Social Work Today*, 22, 18th April

Trotter, J. (1997) 'The Failure of Social Work Researchers, Teachers and Practitioners to Acknowledge or Engage Non-Abusing Fathers: A Preliminary Discussion', *Social Work Education*, 16(2), 63-76.

Trotter, J., Kershaw, S. & Cox, P. (forthcoming) *Feminist Perspectives on Child Sexual Assault*, London: Macmillan.

Tufts' New England Medical Center (1984) 'Sexually Exploited Children: Service and Research Project', in US Department of Justice *Final Report for the Office of Juvenile Justice and Delinquency Prevention*, US Department of Justice.

Tunnard, J. (1991) 'Setting the Scene for Partnership', in Family Rights Group (ed) *The Children Act 1989: Working in Partnership with Families*, London: HMSO.

Valente, M. & Borthwick, I. (1995) 'Sexual Abuse: Using Survivors' Experience to Confront Denial', *Child Abuse Review*, 4, 57-62.

Wagner, W.G. (1991) 'Depression in mothers of sexually abused vs. mothers of nonabused children', *Child Abuse and Neglect*, 15, 99-104.

Waldby, C., Clancy, A., Emetchi, J. & Summerfield, C. (1989) 'Theoretical perspectives on father-daughter incest', in Driver, E. & Droisen, A. (eds) *Child Sexual Abuse*, London: Macmillan.

Wattam, C. (1989) *Child Sexual Abuse: Listening, hearing and validating the experiences of children*, Harlow: Longman.

Wattam, C. & Woodward, C. (1996) '"And Do I Abuse My Children? No.": Learning about prevention from people who have experienced child abuse', in National Commision of Inquiry into the Prevention of Child Abuse (ed) *Childhood Matters*, London: The Statioery Office.

Wells, J. (1992) 'Adult Agendas and Children's Experience - A Response to Secondary Victimization', *Child Abuse Review*, 1, 52-55.

Wetherell, M. (1993) 'Social Structure, Ideology and Family Dynamics: The Case of Parenting', in Wetherell, M., Dallos, R. & Miell, D. (eds) *Interactions and Identities*, Buckingham: Open University Press.

Westcott, H.L. (1993) *Abuse of Children and Adults with Disabilities*, London: NSPCC.

Westcott, H. (1995) 'Perceptions of child protection casework: views from children, parents and practitioners', in Cloke, C. & Davies, M. (eds) *Participation and Empowerment in Child Protection*, London: Pitman.

White, R. (1990) 'Empowerment', *Child Abuse Review*, 4(2), 7-8

Wyatt, G. & Higgs, M. (1991) 'After the Medical Diagnosis: Everyone's Dilemma', in Richardson, S. & Bacon, H. (eds) *Child Sexual Abuse: Whose Problem?*, Birmingham: Venture Press.

# Index

## A
abusers
 family of origin as neglected factor  70
 gender  6
acceptance  55-57
agency responses  40, 83, 94-97
 expectations of fathers  38
 to emergencies  92
AIDS/HIV  17
anger  42-61

## B
Beckford Inquiry  62
black families  63
blame  22-23, 30, 41, 50, 66-68, 69
 by professionals  63

## C
challenging behaviour  91
child sexual abuse  6
 and amnesia  38, 46
 contact issues  90
 definition used  6-7
 disclosure  15-17
 familial and non-familial  87
 long term reactions of parents  57-61
 reluctance to disclose  5
 response of extended families  10-12, 45
 response of non-abusing parents  8, 41-61
  parenting skills  59
Children Act, 1989  25-27
 restrictions on professional action  83
children in care  80-82
Churches  58
client-centred approaches  109
collusion
 by professionals  69

## D
daughters  35
deaf children  84
denial  10, 45-49, 106
disability  3, 73, 75, 84

disclosure 88-90, 109
domestic violence 43

## E
empowerment 115
  of staff 115

## F
families
  conflict within 100
  polarisation of feelings 85
  response to child sexual abuse 85
family disfunctionalists 23, 69
fatherhood 30-32
fathering activity
  and gender of child 34
fathers 28-29
  absence of 31
  agency responses 38-40
  and abuse 35, 37-38, 72
    prevalence 37-38
  and blaming 70
  and child care responsibilities 31, 34-35
  and custody 28
  and 'family system' 34
  as 'alternative mother' 36
  as positive resource 82
  involvement with family 39
  neglected in literature 22-23, 24-27, 29, 31
  research on 36
  rights 31
  roles 30-32, 34
  sampling difficulties 30
  seen as perpetrators 25, 37
feminism 23, 36, 69
forgiveness 58
fratriarchy 33

## G
gender issues 3, 23, 32-33, 34-35
  and power 116-118
grieving 51, 51-55
grieving process 56
group work 58, 77
guilt (of parents) 49-50

## H
heterosexual relationships 31

*Index*

# I
incest 37, 69
Inquiries
  impact on professional practice 76
isolation 11
ivestigations 95

# L
lay people 104-105
lesbian mothers 31, 73, 74
loss 51

# M
male roles 36
masculinity 36
Men's Studies 36
mothers 27-28
  and abused children 24-27, 42
  and blaming 66, 69
    lack of research base 68-73, 69
  and child mental health 27
  and collusion 66, 67
  anger 42
  depression 54
  lesbian mothers 31, 74
  quality of professional support for 64
  stereotyping by professionals 63, 64

# O
observer bias 4

# P
parenting
  social context 21
parents
  abusing and non-abusing 1-2
  non-abusing and abused children 2, 21-23
  parents' views 24
  paucity of literature on non-abusive parents 21
  self-reliance 59
  stereotyping by professionals 107-112
partnership 112
patriarchy 32-33
police 17-20
power imbalances 23-24, 28, 115-118
problem-centred aproaches 109
professional interventions 2, 33, 62
  factors influencing 63

professional practice
  impact of Inquiries  76
professionals  2, 17, 18-20, 24, 39, 48, 53
  and multidisciplinary working  62
  communication with families  97
  discriminatory attitudes of  73-76
  identification with clients  86
  negative interventions  66, 83
  partnership with parents  106-107
  strategies for supporting parents  109-112
psychiatrists  23
psychologists  23

## R

rape  56
research methodologies  3-7, 37, 114
role of parents
  differences between mothers and fathers  23-24, 24-29
    in Children Act, 1989  25

## S

secondary traumatization  41
self help  105-106
self-help  104-106
serial abusers  105
sexuality  31, 74, 79, 80
social services investigations  17-20

## T

therapeutic work  79
  and legal process  79
training
  for non-abusing parents  113-114
  for professionals  112-114
trauma
  of parents  52
traumagenic dynamics  78
treatment  104-107
  effectiveness  104

## V

voluntary organisations  77-78

## W

women
  status of role in caring professions  29